DO WHAT WORKS

DO WHAT WORKS

Smarter Government, Better Results

Edited by Michele Jolin and David Medina

With contributions from bipartisan leaders including Wes Moore, Mike DeWine, Tate Reeves, Rahm Emanuel, Peter Orszag, John Bridgeland, and more

DISRUPTION
BOOKS

Washington, DC

Published by Disruption Books
Washington, DC
www.disruptionbooks.com

Distributed by Disruption Books

For information about special discounts for bulk purchases, please contact Disruption Books at info@disruptionbooks.com.

All proceeds of the sale of this book will be donated to charity.

Cover and book design by Sheila Parr
Cover image used under license from iStockphoto/2170047570

Library of Congress Cataloging-in-Publication Data available

Printed in the United States of America

Print ISBN: 978-1-63331-146-6
eBook ISBN: 978-1-63331-147-3

First Edition

10 9 8 7 6 5 4 3 2 1

To the dedicated public servants—across the country and at every level of government—who are working tirelessly to deliver better results.

CONTENTS

INTRODUCTION

A BETTER WAY EMERGES

PETER ORSZAG, FORMER DIRECTOR OF THE WHITE HOUSE OFFICE OF MANAGEMENT AND BUDGET (OBAMA)

JOHN BRIDGELAND, FORMER DIRECTOR OF THE WHITE HOUSE DOMESTIC POLICY COUNCIL (G. W. BUSH)

Thirteen years ago, the two of us—Peter, a Democrat who served as director of the White House Office of Management and Budget (OMB) under President Barack Obama, and John, a Republican who served as director of the White House Domestic Policy Council under President George W. Bush—teamed up to write a piece for *The Atlantic*. The topic was a shared focus of ours: the federal government's persistent failure to evaluate whether the money it spent was being used effectively.

We titled our essay "Can Government Play Moneyball?"—a reference to the book by Michael Lewis (and the film starring Brad Pitt) about baseball's Oakland Athletics. In 2002, that team—badly outspent by wealthier rivals—adopted an evidence-based approach to player acquisition and development, eschewing the subjective judgments of old-school scouts in favor of hard data and sophisticated analysis. The Athletics found great success with this data-driven approach. And we wondered if government could do the same. At a time when spending decisions were largely being driven by a host of subjective considerations—partisan politics, personal relationships, and pure hunches on the part of policymakers—could our leaders instead use objective data to get a better bang for the taxpayer's buck?

With the support of Results for America—and the partnership of economists, strategists, and elected officials on both sides of the aisle—that article became a book, *Moneyball for Government*. Despite the fact that it was published at a moment when partisan polarization was on the rise, fiscal austerity was at the top of the national agenda, and distrust of government was high, we viewed the book as fundamentally optimistic. Its chapters illustrated that leaders on both sides of the aisle yearned for a better way forward—and the book also described both the specific policies and the broader process changes that would be required to reach that brighter future.

Since then, we have both left government: Peter for the private sector and John for the nonprofit world. And the situation in Washington, from a first glance, doesn't seem to have improved much.

Partisan polarization is the highest it's been in recent decades. Annual budget deficits have grown and continue to grow. Federal debt held by the public as a share of gross domestic product has increased by a third over the last decade.

Perhaps worst of all, political leaders—and the general public—continue to lose faith in the government's ability to be effective. President Donald Trump's Department of Government Efficiency (DOGE) cut swaths of federal government agencies and shrank the civil service, underscoring the broader conservative discontent over the size and scope of the administrative state. At the same time, those on the left fear the erosion of government's ability to address complex social and economic challenges.

In his provocative book *Why Nothing Works: Who Killed Progress—and How to Bring It Back*, Brown University's Marc J. Dunkelman explores government's failure to solve big challenges like the housing crisis or climate change. He blames his fellow progressives for undermining the public confidence required for government to do big things by crippling the powerful institutions required to implement solutions at scale. Distrust of "the establishment," he argues, led progressives to construct safeguards in our political system that, while serving to hold government accountable, also limit government's ability to get stuff done.[1]

Ezra Klein of *The New York Times* and Derek Thompson, a contributing writer at *The Atlantic*, agree with Dunkelman's thesis. "Over the course of the twentieth century," they write in their national bestseller *Abundance*, "America developed a right that fought the government and a left that hobbled it." Their book prompted a widespread debate within liberal circles about whether progressives who believe in government's ability to solve problems are self-sabotaging their own good intentions.

Their thesis, as they describe it, is deceptively simple. "To have the future we want," they write early in *Abundance*, "we need to build and invent more of what we need." But the book is really about the reasons behind our failure to do just that. They blame a progressive approach that, for decades, focused more on subsidizing demand than on expanding supply, because it emphasized helping people afford the things they needed rather than on making sure there was enough supply of those things. "Countless taxpayer dollars," they write, "were spent on health insurance, housing vouchers, and infrastructure without an equally energetic focus—sometimes without any focus at all—on what all that money was actually buying and building." The result: a national crisis of *not enough*. Not enough housing. Not enough clean energy. Not enough public transit. And, ultimately, not enough being done to help people actually get what they need.

This failure, Klein and Thompson argue in an echo of Dunkelman's complaint about progressives feeding into a sense of distrust in government, led to the rise of right-wing populism. They quote political scientists William Howell and Terry Moe who write that "populists don't just feed on socioeconomic discontent. They feed on ineffective government—and their great appeal is that they claim to replace it with a government that is effective through their own autocratic power."[2]

It seems, then, that there is an emerging bipartisan consensus around the idea that government simply doesn't work. Indeed, if a pair of authors were to reprise our *Atlantic* essay today, attempting to capture the bipartisan zeitgeist, the title might have to be something like, "Can Government Do *Anything* Right?"

Who, then, will speak for the defense? Who will stand up for the notion that, even if its critics often have a point about its failure to effectively and efficiently solve Americans' problems, government is still capable of rising to the occasion? And, most importantly, who will shine a light on a path toward re-earning the public trust necessary for government to address today's challenges?

In this book, as in *Moneyball for Government*, we and our fellow authors outline a vision of government that plays the constructive participant, a government capable of doing big things effectively, a government that is worthy of bipartisan public trust. But this time, we aren't settling for a prescriptive that merely outlines what we wish would happen. Instead, the authors of these chapters will take you inside the rooms where this kind of government *is already happening*.

Indeed, it turns out that not only *can* government play Moneyball, as we suggested thirteen years ago, but that taking an evidence-based approach to decision-making offers a recipe for successful governance at a time when such examples are badly needed.

Before we dive into these examples, however, let us take a moment to outline *how* the incipient Moneyball revolution came about.

In many ways, that story begins in 1993, with President Bill Clinton's signing of the Government Performance and Results Act, which provided for "the establishment of strategic planning and performance measurement." (As many authors in this book will remind us, you cannot manage what you do not measure.) President George W. Bush built on that progress with the implementation of the Program Assessment Rating Tool, or PART, through which programs that weren't working could be identified and then either fixed or discontinued. In seven years, PART assessed around one thousand programs.

Getting Congress on board was the next step, and it would be a difficult one. Legislators largely ignored PART's findings. And although, under President Obama, funding for effectiveness research was built into major legislation like the 2009 stimulus bill and 2010's Affordable Care Act, it was included only over the fierce objections of members of Congress who were not used to having the spending they approved measured for impact after it went out the door.

Yet the movement toward evidence-based policymaking didn't let up and, in 2019, President Trump signed into law the bipartisan Foundations for Evidence-Based Policymaking Act—known as the Evidence Act—building on an idea championed by former Republican House Speaker Paul Ryan and Democratic Senator and Appropriations Committee leader Patty Murray. This law embedded data, evaluation, and learning capacities into federal agencies tasked with executing the programs Congress funded.

Finally, under President Joe Biden, the Office of Management and Budget issued new Uniform Grants Guidance that encouraged state, local, and tribal governments to invest federal funds to build the data infrastructure needed to track what works. And while Congress remains the toughest nut to crack, more and more members are getting on board with the Moneyball approach. In 2023, a bipartisan coalition of members formed the What Works Caucus, and recently this group introduced a resolution to create a new Commission on Evidence-Based Policymaking that would help Congress better integrate data and evidence into the legislative process. So even while legitimate concerns exist over whether federal policy has become too divorced from empirical evidence, there are strong pockets of support for the opposite.

When Washington plays Moneyball, it makes a real difference in human terms:

- AmeriCorps' evidence-driven grantmaking led to more than 372,000 students being served by Reading Corps, which has been shown to increase reading fluency by up to one full academic school year.[3]
- The Supplemental Nutrition Assistance Program, or SNAP, has been shown to increase the chances of a child graduating from high school by eighteen percentage points.[4]
- The temporary expansions of the Earned Income Tax Credit (EITC) and the Child Tax Credit reduced child poverty in the United States by nearly half, lifting more than 2 million children above the poverty line.[5]

- PEPFAR—President Bush's initiative to curb the AIDS epidemic in Africa—has reported saving an estimated 26 million lives, while the President's Malaria Initiative has been credited with helping save 11.7 million lives and preventing 2.1 billion malaria cases since 2000.[6]

While some of these programs have faced disruptions or funding cuts, members of both parties have leaned on evidence of effectiveness in fighting to restore these vital services.

To really see the power of Moneyball, though, we need to move beyond Washington. It is the state and local governments where you'll find the true acolytes. Governors, state legislators, mayors, city council members, county commissioners—and their partners in the private and social sectors—are rallying to the cause of results-driven policymaking like never before.

The first two chapters of this book are written by governors who, at first glance, wouldn't appear to have much in common. Wes Moore of Maryland is a proud progressive. Mike DeWine of Ohio is a pragmatic conservative. Moore ran on a vision of government that can help lift children and families out of poverty, DeWine on fiscal responsibility and a promise to rein in spending. Yet they both believe in the power of using data and evidence to guide their decision-making.

The truth is both sides have a tremendous incentive to play Moneyball. Democrats like Moore want the effectiveness and efficiency of government in order to implement their agendas. Republicans like

DeWine want to show that limited government can still deliver the benefits people count on. Neither side benefits when failing investments are allowed to endure, and both have a reason to invest in proven solutions.

That's why, when you look around the country, data-driven policymaking is happening in red states and blue states alike. Colorado, under Democratic Governor Jared Polis, has invested more than $3.3 billion in evidence-based services for its residents over three years, including a universal preschool program that's reaching nearly 70 percent of the state's four-year-olds. Meanwhile, Tennessee, under the leadership of Republican Governor Bill Lee, is using evidence-based budgeting to increase the impact of taxpayer dollars, investing in proven reentry programs that have helped reduce the statewide recidivism rate for former inmates. In health care, education, workforce development—and even in climate change and criminal justice—data-driven policymaking is transforming issue after issue at the state level. And the effect is even more pronounced at the local level, where mayors and their partners have embraced Moneyball at scale.

More than one hundred cities in the United States, Canada, and Latin America have earned Bloomberg Philanthropies What Works Cities Certification for using data to improve residents' lives. To help these local leaders find, fund, and implement what works, Results for America has developed an Economic Mobility Catalog listing more than three hundred examples of governments implementing commonsense, evidence-based solutions.

When a solution works in one place, leaders across the country take notice. For example: Five communities have replicated Providence Talks, which is a program proven to boost early language development, and in chapter 7, you'll read about how Birmingham, Alabama, found, funded, and implemented its own version of the program, tripling the chances of meeting or exceeding kindergarten readiness standards for thousands of children. And as study after study shows high-impact tutoring to be a powerful tool for helping students catch up, jurisdictions everywhere from Chicago to North Carolina to Denver to Florida are launching and sustaining these programs.

Success is contagious across jurisdictions—and even across levels of government. Building on the federal success of expanding the Earned Income Tax Credit (EITC), thirty-one states, the District of Columbia, and Puerto Rico have since enacted their own EITCs. Inspired by the expansion of the federal Child Tax Credit, twelve states have passed refundable child tax credits, ensuring families receive the full benefits even if they have little or no tax liability.

This book is full of stories like these—stories of elected officials and public servants from all ideological perspectives using data and evidence to make better decisions that change people's lives for the better. These stories don't just make a pragmatic argument for effective government; they also make a *moral* one.

As you'll read in the chapters to come, public servants in both parties and at every level of government are engaging in a new, evidence-based approach, often resulting in the kinds of unexpected wins that made the Oakland Athletics (and the very concept of Moneyball) a national sensation. The answer to our original question—can government play Moneyball?—turns out to be *yes*.

What, then, does the future look like for a more effective government—and how can Moneyball help make that possible?

Consider: The Oakland Athletics did not win the World Series in 2002, the year of Moneyball. But the concept of Moneyball prevailed nevertheless, changing the face of baseball forever. Today, every team has a dedicated staff of analysts—known as *sabermetricians*—who track a volume of data that would have dazzled even the nerdiest baseball fans back in 2002. Every major-league ballpark is equipped with sensors that empower these analysts to measure everything from a pitcher's arm slot to the angle of a hitter's swing. New statistics are constantly being developed and propagated—even casual fans now toss around terms like *exit velocity* and *zone rating*. And any team that fails to incorporate even the tiniest measurements into its decisions is likely to be left in the dust.

The data landscape for policymakers has evolved as well. The amount of data available to government analysts grows every year, and the rise of artificial intelligence has made that analysis easier, more affordable, and more powerful than we could possibly have imagined in 2013. Leaders in the corporate and nonprofit sectors are using data to guide their decision-making on everything from how to allocate their budgets to when to require employees to come into the office.

So there is a clear, practical opportunity for leaders in both parties to make effective use of data. But we also see a *political* opportunity for a resurgence in good government.

We should move forward in the spirit of the policymakers you'll meet throughout this book: sustaining and expanding effective programs, leaving room for innovation and trial periods for new ideas that show potential, and being willing to cut or eliminate programs that aren't working.

That, of course, is easier said than done—which is why this book will show you not just *what* these leaders have done but *how* they've done it. This book isn't just a menu of evidence-backed solutions. It's a playbook for navigating the difficult challenge of implementing those solutions in an often-challenging political climate.

In the end, the success or failure of this approach is up to policymakers. But their partners in the private and social sectors can also support a new, more data-driven approach to solving civic problems. And, of course, it's up to voters to demand that their leaders incorporate data and evidence into their decision-making.

Americans of all political stripes want a government that is accountable, efficient, and focused on results. We believe that leaders of both parties have an obligation to deliver that kind of government—and, what's more, we believe that, right now, despite all the noise and doubt, they have an unprecedented opportunity to deliver it.

This year, America celebrates the 250th anniversary of its declaration of independence. As we embark on the next chapter of the American experiment, now is the time to leave behind antiquated policymaking that fails to make use of objective analysis and evolve our style of government to renew the public's faith. We write today in the hope, and in faith, that we can meet the broad ambitions of our people by focusing our government on the simple principle of doing what works.

1

DATA-DRIVEN, HEART-LED

WES MOORE (D-MARYLAND)

Keshawn needed a ride up the hill to school.

He goes to Arundel Elementary School in the Cherry Hill neighborhood of Baltimore City, which serves more than four hundred kids from prekindergarten through second grade. It's housed in a brand-new building. It also happens to be located on top of a steep hill. And on some days, for some parents in the neighborhood—including Keshawn's mom, Shae, who suffers from knee pain—that hill might as well be Mount Everest.

When we spoke to school leaders, they told us that—especially in bad weather—kids would often fail to show up for school simply because they and their parents couldn't make it up the hill on foot. There's a school bus, but it's only available to kids who live more than a mile away. This kind of chronic absenteeism, whatever the cause, is linked to poor academic outcomes, behavioral challenges, and delayed social-emotional development.

Keshawn's story shines a light on the layered problems that children face when growing up in poverty. It's not as though Maryland doesn't invest in public schools. In fact, we've made record investments in K–12 education each year I have been in office. But these investments weren't always reaching the communities in the ways they needed them. And kids like Keshawn in neighborhoods like Cherry Hill—where generations of children have grown up in poverty—are the first to slip through the cracks. The result? Kids can't get to school.

My government in Maryland wanted to try to do things differently.

You often hear people say that poverty is a choice, and it is, but not on the part of the people living in it. It's a choice on the part of policymakers who aren't willing to do the work to invest in solutions that make a difference. The problem wasn't just that we weren't investing enough in anti-poverty solutions. The problem was that our investments weren't delivering results for the communities who needed them.

We needed to transition our fight against poverty to a targeted, place-based investment strategy that would achieve lasting impact. We would follow the data to see which communities are falling through the cracks. Then we'd target state dollars specifically toward those communities. It's wonky. But it works.

In early 2024, I unveiled legislation called the ENOUGH Act (Engaging Neighborhoods, Organizations, Unions, Governments, and Households), a first-in-the-nation, community-driven effort to reduce the number of children living in concentrated poverty. Under the ENOUGH Act, we would take a data-driven look at the neighborhoods in our state where poverty has persisted, uninterrupted, for decades, and ask: *What if we flooded these areas with resources? What would it look like if we took neighborhoods that have been chronically and historically neglected and decided to prioritize them—unapologetically?*

Not only would we target our investments to the neighborhoods that needed them most, but we would put the money directly in the hands of neighborhood leaders. I believe that the people who live in a community are best positioned to lead change in that community. Every community has different needs, and government programs trying to reduce poverty have had mixed results—in large part because they haven't been listening to the people who are most affected. So instead of a rigid state mandate for how ENOUGH Act dollars would be spent, we set up a grant program where community organizations could apply based on specific neighborhood needs. They set up programs that are 100 percent community-led, and we implemented a metric-based accountability system to track the results of these programs for kids and their families.

One of the first communities to become a part of ENOUGH was Cherry Hill, where Keshawn lives. In Cherry Hill, community leaders had already been working hand in hand with the staff at Arundel Elementary School to identify and reach out to families of chronically absent students like Keshawn—not to demand they show up but to ask what was making regular attendance hard. A lack of reliable transportation was, resoundingly, the answer. The school wanted to help, but—between securing a school bus and acquiring the proper licenses for drivers—there were too many hurdles in their way. When community partners came together to strategize on how to address this, they came upon a solution from an unlikely place: The local youth football team had a van that sat idle during the school day. Even better, there were coaches—trusted members of the community—who were already certified to drive students in it.

All they needed was a little funding to get the van up and running, and with funding from the ENOUGH Act, school staff were able to secure use of the van during the day. When they called parents like Shae to offer their kids a ride up the hill, every single family they called took them up on the offer. Almost immediately, we saw results: Schools that had students miss dozens of days every year saw absentee rates plummet into the single digits. And in the 2025–26 school year, they were able to add a second van to their little fleet, meaning thirty kids like Keshawn are now able to count on a ride to school every single day.

Shae no longer has to brave that hill on a bad knee. And Keshawn loves the ride in the van almost as much as he loves school itself. We're seeing results in neighborhoods like Cherry Hill because we invested directly in the people who have the solutions to big challenges like chronic absenteeism—people who just need a little bit of money to turn creative ideas into action.

➡ ➡

Maryland is home to spectacular natural beauty, dynamic industries, and people as talented as they are determined. But for too long, we had been leaving too many people behind.

And that's where the data came in. Our administration's policymaking is data-driven and heart-led—just like it was when I was the CEO of the Robin Hood Foundation, one of the nation's largest anti-poverty organizations. At Robin Hood, we took a scientific approach to fighting poverty and, as governor, I wanted to do the same. I wanted to lean on hard data to show us exactly how we needed to act and to make sure we had core benchmarks in place to illustrate what success looked like. I wanted to be able to show taxpayers that our process was the right one and that our solutions were effective. I wanted accountability. I wanted transparency. Most of all, I wanted results.

This was the thinking when I tasked our government with developing our State Plan. For each series of priorities, we identify a specific strategic goal, isolating a particular problem we want to solve. We then develop the tactics necessary for solving the problem and a set of key performance indicators (KPIs) to track our progress—a mix of measurable inputs, outputs, and outcomes. These KPIs are different for each priority, but they're all in service of the same strategic objectives. We track that progress regularly and reliably, and state and agency leadership report results at meetings of our Maryland Performance Cabinet—a group of cross-agency teams that conduct regular data-driven reviews.

Our goal is to scale these concepts across our entire state government and across every investment in our budget—ensuring that every major funding choice is informed by a clear understanding of what works, whether it's proven right here in Maryland or has demonstrated a track record of results elsewhere.

For example: During my first year in office, I was presented with a list of prison reentry programs in Maryland designed to help formerly incarcerated people rejoin society after they've served their time. I asked my team a simple question: Which of these work? Not how many people they serve, not whether good things happen around them, but which programs actually lead to jobs and cause fewer people to return to prison. We couldn't answer that on the spot.

If we couldn't answer these basic questions—the same questions everyday Marylanders ask of their government—then we had to do more. I want people to be better off, and I want to know whether a program actually made that happen—not just whether it sounded like a good idea but whether it meaningfully improved people's lives. Results, first and foremost, must drive our decisions.

We adopted a statewide definition of "evidence"—so that we're all on the same page when it comes to what we mean by "what works." This results-driven process will enable us to review hundreds of millions of dollars in proposed investments to determine whether or not they have a proven track record of success. And now we're looking to go even deeper by providing indicators of evidence-based investments in public budget documents and moving Maryland from a "performance-informed" past to a national model for evidence-based governance.

Since making these changes, we have invested more than $50 million in programs with a demonstrated track record of success.

That includes programs to help justice-involved young people build safer futures. In 2023, we created the Thrive Academy. We did research—identifying youth who were at the highest risk of perpetrating or being a victim of a violent crime—and surrounded them with intensive supports, like housing, jobs, and food, as well as physical and mental-health plans. A year after we launched Thrive, we saw remarkable results: 80 percent of the youth served are choosing a path beyond the justice system, with zero gun-related rearrests.

This is what we mean when we say we are data-driven and heart-led in the state of Maryland. We are a team of data wonks, yes—but we are also a team of dreamers. And without making a firm commitment to including data in everything we do—and establishing the infrastructure to fulfill that commitment—we know that our best intentions won't amount to a hill of beans.

Through ENOUGH, we are channeling more state money toward communities caught in cycles of poverty. Through data-backed policymaking, we are looking through our balance sheets and making our investments deliver societal returns. But of all the ways we now use data in Maryland, perhaps the most exciting is how data can lead us to new breakthrough policies. Because when you follow the data, you often land on discovery.

The data—both in Maryland and nationwide—shows that our young men and boys are falling behind. Labor force participation for young men is nearly as low as it has been in two decades. Suicide rates among men under thirty have risen by more than a third since 2010. College attainment has stalled at the same level reached in 1964. And in Maryland, we have been sending young men under eighteen to state prison at twice the national rate.

Behind these statistics are real boys and young men who are struggling. I know what they're going through because I've lived it myself. I was one of these young men and boys—not a problem to be solved but a person who needed support. I grew up in a community that was overpoliced and underfunded. When I was three, I watched my dad die in front of me from a health condition that was preventable. At eleven, I felt handcuffs on my wrists. I was sent to military school as a teenager.

I could have gone down a different path, but I found purpose through service. I now find myself as one of the most improbable governors in the country—all because I got my fair shot from my mom, who worked day and night to make it happen. I realize just how much of an impact a fair shot can give to our young men, which is why every action we've taken has been in service of creating opportunities for more Marylanders.

Opportunity was top of mind when we launched a cabinet-level agency dedicated to service and civic innovation, and a first-in-the-nation Service Year Option program to help young people explore career pathways, give back to their communities, and become well-equipped to contribute to Maryland's workforce. It's also why we launched the Thrive Academy.

But this data shows we need a whole-of-government approach to stop the concerning trends we are seeing with young men and boys. So in 2025, I directed my entire administration to implement solutions across the government to help young men and boys.

According to the best evidence available, that means supporting strong families to make sure boys are coming up in good homes. It means preparing more young men for careers—such as teaching—where they can earn a family-sustaining wage and serve as role models for future generations. It means expanding access to mental-health supports and fostering safer, stronger communities where young men can thrive. And it means responding to our struggling young men with care instead of criminalization.

In the crowd at my 2025 State of the State address was a reverend from New Shiloh Baptist Church named Carlos Battle. Carlos is a true community leader, and a member of a nonprofit that connects young men and boys with mentorship opportunities. But back in the early 2000s, he was addicted to cocaine and heroin.

He continued to use, even after he was arrested on a drug charge, and as a result of his addiction he violated the terms of his probation. Under Maryland law at the time, Carlos could never get his record wiped clean, even after he turned his life around.

I introduced legislation to change that, so people like Carlos could petition for expungement. I wanted to build a Maryland where every time residents in Carlos's position applied for a job or a home loan, they wouldn't constantly be shadowed by decisions they made decades ago. A few months later, our state lawmakers responded, passing sweeping reforms to make it easier for Marylanders to clear their records.

We need men like Carlos in our communities to serve as examples for our young boys—and the data tells us exactly how we can make sure these kinds of leaders succeed.

Success stories like that are happening all over Maryland. But it's the ENOUGH Act—the initiative helping Marylanders like Keshawn in Cherry Hill—that's become our signature reform. There, our approach to lifting people out of poverty with a heart full of empathy and a briefcase full of data can be most easily understood.

Instead of spreading money around, we're targeting the places that are most in need of our help. And we're doing it in a way that follows local and national best practices. For years, leaders in the private and philanthropic sectors have been driving change by focusing on places and people. It's time for state government to catch up. ENOUGH isn't just about a renewed focus on poverty—it's about a new way of governing. We believe in following the data. We believe in efficient and effective investment. And most importantly, we believe that the people closest to the problems are also closest to the solutions.

Every community faces unique challenges: a lack of job training, a shortage of transportation, a dearth of health-care providers, unsafe streets, a failure of entrepreneurs to access capital. It would be up to community leaders to come together and create comprehensive plans on how to make their communities better. They would provide the vision—we would provide the funding.

In December 2024, I was able to announce the first round of ENOUGH Act funding: $13.1 million in grants to twenty-seven community-based partnerships in neighborhoods where concentrated poverty is highest. After the first year, we were able to announce an additional $19 million for communities to build on their work. The philanthropic and private sectors stepped up, too, committing more than $100 million in aligned funding to support our work.

The early results show that communities have seen more than a three-to-one return on our initial investment. We've engaged more than twelve thousand Maryland residents through this work, with twenty-seven communities holding a total of more than 1,300 events for us to hear directly from the people we're trying to serve. Communities have built more than 550 sustainable, cross-sector partnerships. And we've implemented more than eighty evidence-led programs to increase access to good jobs, good schools, quality health care, and safe neighborhoods.

Our work is grounded in data. But the results are all about people.

As a student-athlete at South Hagerstown High School, R. J. Franklin dreamed of playing football in college, but the extra training and coaching he would need to get there were out of his reach financially. R. J. is a really smart, driven kid—he just needed a little help. And ENOUGH provided it by way of a program called Cash N' Dreams. Created by San Mar Family and Community Services, the program supports local teenagers in three ways: with financial literacy lessons, interpersonal skills coaching, and direct financial assistance.

R. J. used his grant to enroll in specialized training camps, and, today, he's playing football at Lycoming College in Pennsylvania, where he's slated to graduate with a degree in sociology.

"I probably wouldn't be where I am now without Cash N' Dreams," said R. J. "It really was a blessing."

All across Maryland, communities are leveraging funding from the ENOUGH Act to make a difference.

These communities know what they need—and, under the ENOUGH Act, we're providing the investment necessary to get it.

I've always understood that there's a measure of intentionality that drives concentrated poverty—and that there needs to be a measure of intentionality in how we address it. The same can be said of every challenge our administration faces: health care, education, public safety, housing, affordability, economic development. Blind faith isn't a strategy. Guessing isn't a strategy. Preserving the status quo and hoping everything will turn out OK isn't a strategy. You need to be intentional—you need to follow the data.

We live at a time when our leaders have more access to data than ever before. But for some reason, our politicians continue to make decisions as though we're still in the age of typewriters and card catalogues. In Maryland, we are proving there is a better way—one where data is the starting point, and delivering real results is the end point. We've proven we can do it with budgeting; we've proven we can do it with men and boys; we've proven we can do it with poverty. And together, we will continue to set the standard for how we leverage the power of data to leave no one behind.

2

PLANTING THE SEEDS OF OPPORTUNITY

GOVERNOR MIKE DeWINE (R-OHIO)

I come from a family of optimists.

My grandfather owned a seed company in Yellow Springs, Ohio. He kept on planting trees right up until he died in his mid-eighties. As a kid, I'd watch him stoop to the soil to plant yet another handful of maple seeds and think, *Why? He's never going to live to see those trees grow very tall.* But he planted them anyway. And now our son, John, gets to tap those very maple trees to produce syrup for our family to sell and enjoy.

The prayer of Saint Óscar Romero tells us, "We accomplish in our lifetime only a tiny fraction of the magnificent enterprise that is God's work. [Yet] we plant the seeds that one day will grow . . . [because] we are prophets of a future not our own."[1]

Prophets of a future not our own. If there's a better description of—and inspiration for—public service, I haven't heard it.

Indeed, the future, in my mind, is where the policies of today begin. It's the vision of those tall trees that keeps us planting seeds, the promise of a brighter tomorrow that keeps us hard at work today.

That's especially true when it comes to the signature issue of my administration: creating economic opportunity for all Ohioans. Since the day I took office back in 2019, we've been making targeted investments all across the Buckeye State to ensure that every resident has the tools to live up to their God-given potential and the opportunities to live their version of the American Dream. And while some of the initiatives we've created are just beginning to bear fruit, I'm confident that, because of these investments, Ohio's economy will continue to grow, our businesses will continue to expand, and our workforce will continue to grow stronger.

In addition to that willingness to think long-term, there's another reason we've been able to make smart decisions about our economic future: our reliance on data and evidence. Throughout my administration, we've prioritized embracing technology to make Ohio the heart of innovation—and that innovation begins in our very own budget process. We've modernized our state data systems so we can better evaluate our programs and practices and ensure that the dollars we invest are going to programs that work.

Ohio is now recognized as a national model for incorporating data and evidence into our budget process. And, in this chapter, I want to tell you a little bit about how we've done that. But I also want you to understand the "why" of it all. While the details of our data system might seem a little dry, we employ data in the service of an ambitious and future-focused vision for expanding opportunity throughout our state.

You can't use data and evidence in your policymaking process until you have the tools in place to capture and analyze that information. That's why, early in my tenure as governor, I issued an executive order creating a new digital platform called InnovateOhio. The goal of this platform was simple but powerful: In addition to making our government more accessible to everyday Ohioans, it would allow for a fast, seamless, and secure exchange of data and analytics across our various state agencies. This digital transformation of our government, which I asked then–Lieutenant Governor Jon Husted to help lead, would lay some key foundations for the important work ahead. This work set the stage for the DataOhio Portal and the hiring of the state's first chief data officer.

In half a century of public service—I was a prosecutor, a state senator, a US congressman, a lieutenant governor, a US senator, and Ohio's attorney general before becoming governor—I've made my share of mistakes. And I've found that, nearly every time I find myself wishing I'd done something differently, it's because I didn't have enough information at the time I made the call. I didn't want that to happen as governor.

These early decisions weren't made solely in the interest of efficient governance. We had a big vision for Ohio's future, and we knew we'd need to make changes in order to fulfill that vision.

I'll give you two very different examples of how we're leveraging the power of data to improve outcomes.

First: In November 2019, I announced a new initiative called H2Ohio, which was designed to address the complex issues impacting Ohio's waters. For many years, excess phosphorus runoff from Ohio's farmlands was a leading contributor to both lower water quality and harmful algal blooms on Lake Erie. Meanwhile, our water infrastructure—from the pipes that carry drinking water to our taps to septic systems that carry away waste—was aging and, in many cases, failing. We collected as much information as we could, consulted experts from different perspectives, followed the science, and then took action: implementing incentives for farmers to adopt sustainable nutrient-runoff practices, creating more wetlands, investing in infrastructure funding in underserved communities, and taking care of potential lead exposures in our schools and day care centers. The data gave us direction, and we worked with our partners in the legislature to secure $172 million in funding.[2]

Today, more than three thousand Ohio farmers are following best practices to reduce nutrient runoff on more than 2.5 million acres of farmland.[3] Additionally, more than two hundred wetlands across Ohio have been built or restored to improve our waterways and landscapes by filtering out nutrients before they cause problems in our water.[4] The Ohio Department of Agriculture estimates a phosphorus reduction of 532,000 pounds based on 2024 completed practices.[5] Additionally, the wetlands supported by the Ohio Department of Natural Resources reduce 41,308 pounds of phosphorus per year in the Western Lake Erie Basin.[6]

Second: I've always been concerned about the health of our youngest Ohioans, and the data illustrates clearly that two major causes of death for infants are being born too early and not sleeping in a safe environment. We've invested in maternal health with a focus on reducing premature births, and dramatically expanded our home-visiting program, where professionals come directly to the homes of new parents to help serve as critical supports in those exhausting early days. In places where programs like these have been implemented, investigations by Child Protective Services have decreased by 44 percent, and mothers showed a 30 percent drop in postpartum depression.[7]

Data and evidence go into every decision we make—and they're behind every dollar we choose to spend.

When we issued our first budget guidance, we required state agencies to submit logic models with their requests, explaining exactly what outcome they were expecting to achieve in exchange for their funding.

Not everyone got the hang of it right away. In those first years, we had to send back some submissions where agencies treated increased funding itself as the desired outcome. *No*, we had to explain, sometimes more than once, *we need to understand the outcome for Ohioans.*

It was a culture change—and, frankly, at first it was a bit of a culture shock. But today, there's a chief data officer at every one of our state agencies, and now our leaders across state government are learning to demonstrate outcomes instead of just looking at outputs.

We also use data ourselves to tell Ohio's story. For example: Usually, when you're seeking a AAA credit rating, you fly out to New York with a PowerPoint and meet with the rating agencies. Instead, we brought them to us, inviting them to visit Ohio so we could show them the data we'd collected not just on our own results, but on how we compared to other AAA-rated states. We earned the AAA rating we were looking for, allowing us to engage in capital projects at a lower interest rate and continue investing in what works.

The reorientation of our state's government around data and evidence made it easier for us to tackle our signature challenge: making Ohio the nation's best place to start or grow a business.

I spend a lot of time recruiting companies to come to the Buckeye State. And the same question always comes up. No matter what I tell CEOs about our low tax and stable regulatory environment, and no matter how much I brag about our natural resources and unbeatable quality of life, they invariably ask: "Are you going to be able to fill the jobs?"

This is what we call a "good problem"—because the truth is that Ohioans are ready to seize these opportunities. They just need a little help removing the roadblocks that slow them down. That's why my administration has taken an evidence-backed approach to producing enough qualified workers to meet the needs of our business community.

For example: By the time I took office in 2019, it was clear that the *kinds* of jobs companies were looking to fill were changing. Like many industrial states, our economy was being disrupted by the technological revolution. And our workforce development system just wasn't keeping up.

You can't train a worker for a new career overnight, let alone thousands and thousands of workers. But we needed to make that training as speedy, and as accessible, as possible. The data was clear that educational pathways requiring years of postsecondary study were both too slow and, for many students, so expensive as to be completely out of reach. What we needed was a way to upskill people quickly, no matter their economic circumstances.

The TechCred program has been key to workforce development. Established in my first year as governor, this bipartisan initiative created a credential training reimbursement program. Employers front the money to upskill their employees, and the state reimburses them up to $2,000 per credential. Right away, the program was a hit. In the first sixteen months, more than 23,000 credentials were funded at more than 1,300 employers.[8] Within a few years, TechCred became a cornerstone of our workforce strategy: In November 2025, for example, we awarded a record-setting $14 million in TechCred funding.[9]

Rallying our existing workforce was an important step forward. But we also knew we had to address the "brain drain" that was letting too much of our homegrown talent depart for other states. We couldn't afford to squander the opportunity presented by our brilliant and creative young people.

We began by looking at the data, which showed that around 60 percent of students in the top 5 percent of their graduating classes were staying in Ohio for postsecondary education.[10] We set the goal of increasing that number to 65 percent. To get there, we introduced the Governor's Merit Scholarship, a program providing $5,000 a year for four years to students at the top of their classes who committed to attending a participating institution here in Ohio.

Because we kept close track of the data, we were able to see and measure the results—and they surpassed our expectations. Instead of reaching 65 percent, we hit 75 percent and kept on going up with each successive year.[11] Today, there are counties in Ohio where every single student to whom we make this offer accepts. And, overall, there are thousands of brilliant young people currently in Ohio colleges who might have gone elsewhere if not for the help we've been able to provide.

I often think of the example of Ellie Baker, one of the first Ohio seniors to receive the scholarship. She was valedictorian of her class at Claymont High School in Tuscarawas County and could have gone anywhere for college. But if she'd left Ohio, we might not have ever had the chance to get her back. Because of our scholarship, she chose to attend Kent State University. Ellie told us later, "I come from Appalachia, a historically low-income area, where paying for college isn't the easiest thing. However, I didn't want that to hold me back from achieving my aspirations."

Years from now, young Ohioans like Ellie could be launching businesses right here in the Buckeye State—because of a data-backed investment we made today.

Meanwhile, we're incentivizing our colleges and universities to be more active partners in developing tomorrow's workforce by partially tying funding to student outcomes—including how many graduates are able to find employment. We're the first state in the nation to do so.

We're even integrating career planning into existing high school curricula to help students map out their goals and identify what kind of postsecondary training or education they might need to achieve them. And over the last four years, we've seen a 10 percent growth in the number of students participating in career tech—that's more than thirteen thousand additional students earning credentials and engaging in career tech education than were doing so in 2021.[12]

One of those students is named Drew Corbitt. Drew was an excellent student at Jonathan Alder High School in Plain City, Ohio. He played sports and was an active member of the school community. When his mother, Cathy, started working at Tolles Career & Technical Center, she gently—but firmly—nudged Drew to apply to Tolles for engineering. At first, he wasn't thrilled about leaving his friends for two and a half hours a day, but he trusted his mom and, after recognizing that he could still stay involved in his extracurricular activities at school, he decided to make the investment in his own future.

During his senior year, Drew got a great-paying internship at Hikma Pharmaceuticals in Columbus, where he was able to obtain real-world work experience, solidifying his choice to continue his education right here in Ohio at the University of Cincinnati.

There's so much more we can do—so much more we are doing—to identify and remove obstacles to opportunity for all of our people: people returning from incarceration, people who are living with disabilities, people recovering from substance abuse issues, people in our senior community, and more. And whether it's upskilling our existing workforce, striving to retain homegrown talent, recruiting new workers into Ohio, or unlocking the chance to participate in our economy for all of our citizens, what begins with data can often turn into something truly inspiring: the fulfillment of our vision of an Ohio where opportunity is available to everyone.

Some of these seeds may not bear fruit until after I've left office. But when I travel around the state, I see progress. Businesses are taking note—recognizing the value of starting a business in Ohio and taking advantage of our innovative workforce development initiatives to staff those jobs.

In Defiance County, First Quality Tissue is bringing on four hundred more workers. In Wyandot County, a new soybean processing plant will create over a hundred new jobs. In Lorain County, Ford Motor Company is doubling the workforce at its assembly plant in Avon Lake, providing jobs for another two thousand Ohioans.[13]

Overall, since I took office, we've added more than 124,000 private sector jobs. And over 5.7 million Ohioans are employed in our workforce—we have been at or near records for most of the past year.

Fifteen years ago, CNBC placed Ohio thirty-fourth in the nation in a ranking of the best states to conduct business. Today, we're up to number five nationally, and we're first among our neighboring states.[14]

Our taxes are as low as they've been in half a century. We've trimmed nearly a thousand regulations from our administrative code. Our water is cleaner. Our children are healthier. Our workforce is stronger. Our people are thriving.

But for all the wins we've been able to celebrate, the best wins are the ones yet to come. We owe it to all our young people to open all the awesome and life-changing opportunities that Ohio has to offer. After all, they're our future—our hope for tomorrow. They are the legacy we leave behind.

And so we continue to plant seeds, always mindful that we are prophets of a future not our own.

3

KEEPING YOUR EYE ON THE SCOREBOARD

MAYOR MIKE JOHNSTON (D-DENVER)

ROSANNE HAGGERTY, PRESIDENT AND CEO, COMMUNITY SOLUTIONS

It was the fall of 2023, and the entire city of Denver was on a mission to bring one thousand unhoused residents indoors by the end of the year. I (Mike) had based my spring mayoral campaign on this promise and launched the effort with an emergency declaration on my second day in office in July. For months, the city had been providing regular updates on the drive to one thousand via a public dashboard. The media and the public alike checked the dashboard religiously, as if it held the score of a Denver Broncos game. But each number on the website represented someone brought in from the streets, into warmth and safety. Hotels were repurposed. And the city made furious plans to stand up "tiny-home villages"—microcommunities where dozens of people could live, surrounded by wraparound services to help make their transitions off the streets permanent.

In the end, it came down to one site—and one fateful Zoom call.

The goal of one thousand was slowly coming into view as the weather turned cold. But the deadline of December 31 was quickly approaching. And soon it became clear that meeting the benchmark would hinge on the opening of a single site at the corner of East 38th Avenue and Peoria Street, where a tiny-home community was planned with enough room for more than fifty formerly unhoused Denverites. "We'll be able to go directly into encampments," my senior advisor for homelessness promised a local news station, "and bring people that were living on the streets, in tents, into a home of their very own."

Fifty-four prefabricated mobile shelters were ordered from a company called Pallet. So far, so good. But then somebody noticed a flaw in the design of the community building that would anchor the tiny-home community—the place where meals would be served and other services would be provided. It was the roof—it wasn't going to meet snow load and wind load requirements.

Denver's winters are notoriously cold and snowy. The building simply wouldn't work. And suddenly, the fate of this pivotal tiny-home community was in question.

That's when the message went out from city hall: *We're going to build our own community building.* It was, on its face, an insane proposition. No way could a whole new building be designed, approved, built, and opened in the short time remaining before the new year. But the project engineer, Cara Sequino—with the full weight of the mayor's office behind her—wouldn't take no for an answer. She sent out an invitation—a summons, really—for a Zoom call that would convene every single stakeholder: an architect, the construction company, the chief building official, the project manager from the Department of Transportation and Infrastructure, all the regulatory agencies, and the Department of Housing Stability.

"One hour," Cara said. "We've got one hour."

They turned out not to need the full hour. With all the parties logging on—including me to make sure things moved—the call was wrapped up with two minutes to spare. In the wake of what would go down in city history as "The 58-Minute Meeting," the building was designed and ushered quickly through the city's approval process—a process that was expected to take approximately eighteen months but that was completed in about four weeks. The community opened on New Year's Eve. People moved in. Their former encampment was closed.

And the city of Denver met its goal.

This is the story of how one American city set out on a data-driven effort to end homelessness—one encampment at a time, one newly housed resident at a time, one population at a time. It's the kind of effort many would tell you is impossible at a time when homelessness is on the rise nationally. But Denver's story is instructive not just because it has achieved success in the face of doubts, but because of *how* that success was achieved: with a relentless focus on results, a willingness to embrace new solutions, a commitment to solving one piece of the problem at a time, and an eye always on the scoreboard.

Indeed, Denver's story can be the story of any American city. All you need to replicate it is the right approach, a healthy measure of political will, and some quality data.

For policymakers and the social sector alike, tackling homelessness has always been considered something of an uphill battle. We'd point to three reasons why.

First: Homelessness isn't caused by any one thing. It's driven by a wide range of underlying factors from broader economic insecurity and housing market fluctuations to addiction and mental health challenges. It's the result of a convergence of forces, each with its own set of inputs. This is the kind of problem we're not typically good at solving.

Second: Homelessness, in all its complexity, can't be ended with a single program or by a single entity. At the government level, successfully tackling homelessness implicates housing departments, health departments, social service agencies, and more. And while governments, unlike nonprofits, may have in the building all the players necessary to circle the problem, it's a challenge to get them lined up on the field at the same time. You need the buy-in and coordination of a host of agencies and individual leaders who are used to working in siloes—not an easy challenge for any leader.

Third, and most uncomfortably: Homelessness is extremely visible in a community, and often that makes it a very controversial issue to tackle. If you want to end homelessness, you're inevitably going to be bringing homeless individuals off the streets and into neighborhoods where people are often resistant to that kind of change. So if you want to make it a priority, you must have not just the financial resources but a healthy store of political capital—and an appetite for political risk.

All of these challenges have contributed to a false narrative about homelessness. Too many leaders consider it to be an impossible problem to solve.

And, to be frank, you can look at the data and choose to feel pessimistic. In 2024, the last year for which the US Department of Housing and Urban Development had statistics as of this writing, more than 770,000 Americans were counted as homeless.[1] That count, of course, inevitably missed some unhoused individuals. And it doesn't include those crashing with family or friends because they lack a place of their own. But even that limited count represented an 18.1 percent increase over 2023—a year in which the rate also rose (in that case by 12 percent).

Still, while homelessness remains a significant challenge across America, there are signs of hope and examples of progress. Veteran homelessness, for example, is now at a record low, having fallen by 7.5 percent since 2023.[2] And in more than a dozen communities following an innovative approach that focuses on using data to get people off the streets and into housing as quickly as possible, chronic veteran homelessness is now at zero.[3] Thousands of people are coming in off the streets every year—and systems are being rebuilt to help catch people before they fall.

Mike and I (Rosanne) were introduced by a mutual friend. We quickly bonded over our shared belief that homelessness *is* solvable and a shared commitment to ending the crisis in Mike's beloved city of Denver.

What does it mean to end homelessness in practice? Answering this question has traditionally been more difficult than you might think. For one thing, it requires knowing the actual dimensions of the problem and having good enough data to know, as quickly as possible, whether a community's efforts are succeeding. Assembling that information requires unusual levels of collaboration and rigor. And homelessness is dynamic—it changes every day. Many people experience it as a temporary phenomenon and solve it themselves. Matching individuals or families to what they need to get back on their feet requires judgment and having the right resources available. But we can aim to minimize the number of people experiencing homelessness at any one time. We can make their time on the streets as brief as possible. And we can make homelessness rare and brief across a community by understanding that "ending" homelessness is an ongoing process of preventing, detecting, and resolving housing crises so that they never turn into chronic homelessness.

We call it *functional zero* when a community reaches the point where the number of people experiencing homelessness on any given night does not exceed the number of people exiting homelessness over the course of that month.

Why is it so important to align around a shared, easily understood—and easily measured—definition of success? Well, for one thing, it focuses the key leaders, funders, and the public on a clear goal. Communities often get started on this outcomes-focused approach by first aiming at reaching functional zero among a subgroup, like veterans or youth, then broadening out to reduce homelessness overall.

A goal like functional zero also solves one of the traditional problems with attacking homelessness. Funders—in both the public and social sectors—have tended to evaluate success based on the performance of individual programs. But it takes a whole community to get to zero, including funders taking into account the role they play in contributing to a single community-wide strategy.

That's why Community Solutions—the organization that I lead—developed the Built for Zero model. It measures success not by the outcome of any one program, but by whether a community's entire effort is yielding reductions in homelessness. Under the Built for Zero model, leaders are able to rapidly test new ideas and, with the rigorous use of data, quickly understand whether or not those ideas are working.

The Metro Denver Homeless Initiative (MDHI) has been part of the Built for Zero network since 2015. Metro Denver is a big place, a seven-county area with a total population of 3.2 million people across forty different municipalities. Some of the area is urban and progressive; some of it is rural and conservative. And, at first, the region struggled to achieve quality data and establish coordinated systems across the entire "continuum of care."

I (Mike) was no stranger to that struggle when I decided to run for mayor of Denver in 2023. I had spent eight years in the Colorado State Senate, and later led a bipartisan coalition to pass Colorado's first-ever statewide ballot measure for affordable housing, securing $300 million a year in funding and key regulatory reforms to make the state's housing market more flexible and user-friendly.

Maybe most importantly, however, my background was in education. As a teacher, a principal, and a nonprofit leader, I had learned to make data and evidence central to my work—and I was drawn to the Built for Zero model's focus on person-specific data to end homelessness.

Still, in 2023, that felt like an impossible challenge for Denver. The homeless population had gone up 300 percent in the previous four years.[4] The city was covered in encampments, with tents blocking the entrances to businesses and residents feeling unsafe going to places like hospitals, churches, and post offices. Meanwhile, Denver was coming off a year in which both the crime rate and the occurrence of fentanyl overdoses had risen to record highs.[5] The city was in crisis.

Yet I insisted on campaigning on a promise to end homelessness in my first term. And when I won, I used my inaugural speech to urge citizens to align around that vision. "Every problem is solvable," I said, "and we are the ones to solve them."

My plan began the very next day when I signed an emergency declaration on unsheltered homelessness. This action immediately mobilized city agencies around it as a top priority—instead of taking months to get settled in, the new administration would be in attack mode from day one. It also galvanized the city's attention, signaling to residents that the new mayor was going to move at a pace that required urgency. But while I was making it clear that I took the challenge of ending homelessness seriously, it remained to be seen whether residents would support that approach to tackling that challenge.

A bit of background: For decades, the dominant theory among housing advocates was that people experiencing homelessness should have to effectively *earn* a place to live by participating in treatment or residential programs. But the fact remains that the best, most immediate way to end homelessness for an individual is to give that individual a home. This can be a controversial idea. Homelessness often rides alongside issues like addiction that aren't fixed when someone moves indoors and, to someone who has never experienced homelessness, it might seem futile, even counterproductive, to house a person experiencing issues that might someday land them right back on the streets.

But what Rosanne and I both understood is that "Housing First," as it's known among advocates, doesn't mean housing *only*. It includes supportive services—and, what's more, it makes them more available to people by locating those services in the places where they live. This isn't just a moral stand but a practical one. Yes, Housing First advocates believe that housing should be seen as a basic human right, and Housing First supports the idea that people experiencing homelessness are worthy of safety and dignity no matter what else is happening in their lives—but also, people are better able to make progress elsewhere in their lives if they have a safe, stable place to live.

There's a wealth of evidence showing that Housing First programs work. An overwhelming majority of people who enter these programs stay housed, and making support and services voluntary—as opposed to a condition to be met before housing is allotted—makes it more, not less, likely that people will actually take advantage.

Housing First programs also reduce interactions with institutions like hospitals, jails, and shelters, resulting in cost savings for communities. And in one large, multiple-site research trial, researchers found that the cost of a Housing First program that was paired with intensive case management services was offset by *half* due to the reduced use of shelter visits, emergency departments, and other crisis services.[6]

With this evidence in hand, our team in the mayor's office began implementing a plan to move people indoors as quickly as possible. And at the core of this plan was developing four kinds of housing units: existing rental units that could be sourced and leased, hotels that could be converted into housing, tiny-home villages and other kinds of microcommunities, and large commercial buildings like unused schools, churches, or warehouses.

This approach would be paired with a crackdown on public encampments. The city already had a camping ban on the books, but no longer would it simply shuffle people off one block at a time. Instead, it would move people from encampments into housing—and then close those encampments permanently.

An end to the encampments was a popular idea. Moving unhoused people into neighborhoods across the city was less so. After announcing the plan, I embarked on a town hall tour to sell a Housing First approach to homelessness in Denver, hosting some sixty events within the first six months of my administration. These events often felt like professional wrestling matches, with me and my team cast as the villains—merely walking out onto the stage often resulted in a chorus of boos.

At one town hall, a Denver resident approached me to curse me out—not a totally uncommon experience during this tour. "You're going to kill this neighborhood," the man thundered. "Why are you targeting our community?" Six months later, when the city finally opened the tiny-home village it had been planning in that area, the same resident was there—helping people move in. In those six months, his fears had been assuaged: The homes looked dignified, blended in well with the design of the neighborhood, and felt safe. The process allowed residents like him to find the humanity that had been lurking beneath their apprehension.

There was a lesson there: If you persevere through the hard political decisions early on, you can deliver results that change public opinion—and open up room for further progress.

To be sure, the process was not without challenges and setbacks. In the initial planning, the team had anticipated relying more heavily on tiny-home villages and less on hotels. But once they started to do the math, they realized that, even if each tiny-home village contained fifty housing units, they would still need to find twenty sites in order to house one thousand people. And residents, it turned out, simply felt differently about the creation of a new housing site than they did about hotels—buildings they often drove past without a second thought as to who was inside. Housing people there didn't generate the same level of concerns.

Ultimately, however, Denver found success by following the path the Community Solutions team had constructed when we developed the Built for Zero model.

Setting a clear goal around which people could organize was just one of the ways in which the city was following that model. Borrowing a page from NASA, we assembled a homelessness "tiger team" with top officials from agencies across the city government. We all met on a regular basis at a conference table in the mayor's office, with a war-room feel that kept every department head feeling engaged and accountable. "I don't do homelessness," one agency head said at the outset of the process. The answer? *Well, you do now.*

Meanwhile, a team of dozens of outreach workers fanned out through the city to gather real-time—and, critically, person-specific—data on the unhoused population. As Community Solutions had found in cities across the country, it was essential that these outreach workers get to know each individual—it was important to learn whether they had pets or a partner or special needs. In order to convince people to come indoors, these outreach teams had to be flexible, empathetic, and creative in finding solutions to accommodate each individual's situation. The approach paid off: Within a year and a half of the mayor's program beginning, Denver became the first major city in America to end the cycle of street homelessness for veterans. And, overall, Denver reduced street homelessness by more than 45 percent—more than any other American city in history—bringing 1,200 housing units online in less than six months.

Having met its goal—in dramatic fashion—for 2023, the city launched a new initiative called All In Mile High that would aim to move two thousand people indoors over the course of 2024 while achieving functional zero homelessness for veterans. We met that goal, too, with room to spare, and closed hundreds of blocks' worth of encampments permanently. By early 2026, street homelessness was down 64 percent, and the city achieved its first reduction in overall homelessness in nine years, falling 12.5 percent from the previous year. Denver isn't at functional zero overall yet, but we're well on our way.

In less than two years, Denver went from a city that swept people from block to block to one that treats people with dignity and delivers real results. But this success isn't a miracle, it's just an effective model. And it can be followed by other cities.

We would humbly offer a few pieces of well-earned advice to city leaders looking to replicate Denver's success.

First: Housing First is impossible without housing. You cannot solve the problem unless you're able to bring on enough units of housing—quickly and affordably. Which means you can't wait until it's feasible to build $700,000 single-family homes for each individual. Getting units up and running is the name of the game, and you need to see the path to sufficient housing in order to make a measurable impact.

Second: Housing First doesn't mean housing *only*—you need to make additional support not just available, but accessible. Decentralizing services is a critical strategy for solving homelessness. If all the wraparound services are located in the city center, that's where unhoused people will cluster. Instead, spread those services around your city so people can access them at multiple sites.

Third: You need buy-in from the community. Realize that solving homelessness is fundamentally about safety—both for the unhoused and for the housed. And every step you take has to make both parties feel safer. In Denver, whenever we got people off the streets, we would close down encampments permanently and invest resources into making sure they didn't reappear. The problem, once solved, stayed solved. And as residents began to see the streets clear, they got on board with what we were doing.

Fourth (and this piece of advice applies to issues across the spectrum): It's important to be obsessed with outcomes and not processes. You have to start with a clear, ambitious goal and then work backward to figure out the best way to achieve it. And by tracking your progress toward that goal in an accountable way—like with Denver's public dashboard—you can discard processes that aren't working and double down on those that are.

Finally, a word about narrative.

If people don't believe in their guts that homelessness is solvable, they won't support the work necessary to solve it. Despair is the enemy when it comes to problems like these. Yet so much of the media coverage of homelessness focuses on what's not working. We see so many pictures of encampments, read so many stories about mental health challenges and addiction and urban blight. There's almost a cloud of disbelief around the idea that real progress can be made.

We need to tell a new story about homelessness—one that acknowledges the scale of the problem and the impact it has on individuals and communities but also highlights the fact that cities across the country are making real progress in solving it. More than a dozen cities have achieved functional zero for at least one population—not as a onetime achievement but as a sustained reality, and more than forty communities in the Built for Zero movement have achieved measurable reductions.

In big cities and small towns alike, advocates are implementing the model developed by Community Solutions to make a real impact. By telling the story of places like Denver, we can do more than just highlight progress—we can inspire others to take action. Making homelessness rare and brief in our time is really possible. We know what works. Now what we need is the will to move forward along the path cities like Denver have forged.

4

THERE'S NO SUCH THING AS A MIRACLE

GOVERNOR TATE REEVES (R-MISSISSIPPI)

CAREY WRIGHT, FORMER MISSISSIPPI SUPERINTENDENT OF EDUCATION

"Thank God for Mississippi."

As a Mississippian, I've grown up hearing people from across the country invoke this phrase to stereotype and put our state down. But let me tell those people something: This isn't your grandfather's Mississippi.

Today, Mississippi has unprecedented momentum. And in the classroom, Mississippi isn't making news—we're making history. People from across America are taking notice of the special things happening here, and the "Mississippi Miracle" is the envy of the nation. In fact, when people talk about how to improve public education, Mississippi is now seen as the blueprint.

While our nation-leading education gains are often called the Mississippi Miracle, it really wasn't inexplicable at all. It was the result of a deliberate and intentional effort to get Mississippi off the bad lists and onto the good lists in education through effective public policy reforms and implementation. It started more than a decade ago and the results have been worth it.

I (Tate) was elected lieutenant governor in November of 2011. I came to office with a simple philosophy reflecting our state's conservative values: I believe that the most important thing a government can do is to make sure every citizen can find success without *relying* on the government. That means everyone should be able to find a job that allows them to take care of themselves and raise a family. There are very few problems the government works on that couldn't be solved by the individual—if that individual has the skills and opportunities to get a job that pays a decent wage. Of course, that's impossible without a solid education that prepares people for meaningful careers.

Now, I'm a product of the public education system and a proud graduate of Florence High School. Based on my own education experience, I never believed Mississippi's schools were as bad as people made them out to be. But when I took office in January of 2012, there was definitive data that suggested we needed to breathe new life into an education system that had fallen behind. We were at the bottom of the national rankings. At the heart of the problem was an uncomfortable reality: As a state, we just weren't doing a good enough job of teaching our kids how to read.

Fourteen years later, all that's changed. Mississippi has drastically turned around its education system, and our students are learning more than ever before. In 2013, Mississippi's fourth graders were forty-ninth in America for reading. Now, they are ninth. In 2013, Mississippi's fourth graders were fiftieth in the nation for math. Now, they are sixteenth.[1]

Perhaps even more impressive is that we're not just helping some students, in some districts. Our reforms are helping all of Mississippi's students, in all of Mississippi's districts.

As an example, in 2013, Mississippi's African American students ranked forty-fifth compared to their peers. Today, they are third. When compared to their peers around the country, Mississippi's Hispanic students are first in America in reading and second in math.[2] Those are life-changing improvements.

Once we improved the results, it was easy to increase the money we spent on educators. Teachers' pay raises have flowed generously in Mississippi—because we have better results.

Today, states all over the country are wondering how Mississippi managed to do it. We're proud of our historic results, and we encourage other states to follow our lead. We want every state to be able to experience its own version of the Mississippi Miracle. We have the formula. It is a result of effective public policy reforms and implementation, high expectations, continuous improvement—and following the evidence wherever it leads.

Now, if you don't know much about Mississippi politics, the position of lieutenant governor might not seem like that powerful of an office. You probably imagine the lieutenant governor just going to a lot of ribbon cuttings and giving speeches to empty ballrooms. But in our state, the office offers a real opportunity to drive change. Here's why: The lieutenant governor is the presiding officer of the state Senate. They have the power to appoint every member of every committee, including the committee chairs who decide which bills get to move forward. And so, I had the opportunity to appoint the chair of the education committee—the point person who would help me drive forward the reform agenda we'd campaigned on.

I appointed Gray Tollison, a state senator from Oxford who had been a longtime Democrat before switching parties. Like me, Gray believed that education was one arena where government had a real role to play in ensuring success for every child. And while it was a controversial selection, I knew I could count on Gray to be an effective partner. Together, we got right to work, drawing up and passing a series of reforms that would lead to the Mississippi Miracle.

One of the biggest misconceptions about the Mississippi Miracle is that it is a result of one decision. It is not. It stems from a series of reforms that we passed and implemented.

In 2012 and 2013, the Mississippi Legislature acted boldly to reform our state's education system. It was during that time that we instituted Education Scholarship Accounts (ESAs) for our students with special needs, allowed students in failing districts to go to public charter schools, and consolidated districts to get more money into the classrooms.

We also changed the way we rated school districts by creating a simplified *A*, *B*, *C*, *D*, or *F* rating system, so parents could easily understand whether their local school was performing up to par. This played a huge role in increasing accountability.

Additionally, until I took office, Mississippi was one of the only states in the nation that *elected* its school superintendents. I thought that was nuts. When you need to hire a football coach, you don't elect one of the townspeople—you go out and find the best person for the job. So we changed the rules: Going forward, school districts would elect local boards of education, and those boards would be vested with the power to hire the individual who was most qualified to serve as superintendent.

In 2013, we also passed one of the most consequential pieces of legislation in Mississippi's history: the Literacy-Based Promotion Act (LBPA). When we started drafting the LBPA, we knew it wouldn't be easy. The education establishment resisted it. They said new money was the answer and not new ideas. They said passing the LBPA would be disastrous for students, and that we were setting them up for failure.

But I firmly believed that if we focused on the fundamentals, like phonics, raising standards and accountability, and teacher and student support, we could improve the trajectory of education throughout Mississippi. And that's exactly what happened.

The idea behind the bill was simple. We said that from pre-K through third grade, Mississippi students should be learning to read. But once they get to the fourth grade, they'd better be reading to learn. If you can't read, you can't pass. It really was as simple as that.

Mississippi said "no" to social promotion. Under the LBPA, third graders would get multiple opportunities to pass a basic reading test, and if they couldn't, they'd be held back for another year in third grade.

This so-called third-grade gate was controversial. Nobody likes to think about kids being held back. But we believed that, if we raised the level of expectations, Mississippians would rise up to meet them. They ended up exceeding them.

Of course, it wasn't fair to just demand better without providing students and teachers with the resources to execute on the plan. As lieutenant governor, I demanded that we back up the LBPA with real support. That's why we invested in literacy coaches and professional development. And we made sure educators, parents, and students had time to prepare before it went into effect.

The LBPA also called on schools to start screening kids at a young age so we could catch any literacy problems early. Kids who needed extra help would get access to special services so they could catch up. The bill also directed schools to create an Individualized Reading Plan for every struggling student, bringing parents and teachers together to fill in any remaining gaps.

But maybe one of the most significant things the LBPA did was bring a long-overdue end to a major debate over what *kind* of reading education was best for our kids.

People have been arguing about this for *decades*. On one side, you've got folks who believe in teaching phonics—a system where kids learn the relationship between individual letters and the sounds they make so they can put them together to make words. On the other, you've got folks who believe in teaching a "whole language" approach, where kids learn to recognize sight words and use context clues to figure out the ones they don't know.

The argument has always been fierce. Horace Mann, known to some as the "father of American education," was a big whole language guy. About phonics, he once raged, "There stands in silence and death, the stiff, perpendicular row of characters, lank, stark, immovable, without form or comeliness, and, as to signification, wholly void. They are skeleton-shaped, bloodless, ghostly apparitions; and hence it is no wonder that the children look and feel so deathlike when compelled to face them."[3]

Here's the thing, though: Research has shown that one side is right, and it isn't Horace Mann's. In 1997, Congress formed the National Reading Panel, a coalition of experts focused on assessing what the data had to say about the question. Their conclusion, delivered in a 2000 report, was clear and unambiguous: Teaching phonics works.[4] Indeed, a new concept soon emerged: the Science of Reading. This approach focuses on five research-supported components: phonemic awareness (the ability to identify sounds and combine them to form words), phonics, fluency, vocabulary, and comprehension.

You can still travel around the country and find people with different perspectives on whole language vs. phonics vs. some kind of middle-ground approach that tries to have it both ways. But as far as Mississippi is concerned, the debate was settled with the passage of the LBPA, which requires that all schools follow the Science of Reading approach. (Many other states have since passed similar requirements.)

Not everyone was happy with our decision. I imagine Horace Mann rolled over in his grave. But I was committed to following the science on this one, and the data, to me, was overwhelming and convincing. If we were going to get this right, we had to let the research and data guide us, and that's exactly what we did.

Having gotten the LBPA signed into law, our next job was to get it implemented successfully—and that meant finding a new superintendent of education to lead that implementation.

In Mississippi, that's an advice-and-consent position, meaning the state Senate would have to approve of our choice. And when we first started talking up Carey—an East Coaster who'd never worked or even lived in Mississippi—there was a little bit of a political uproar. A lot of folks in Mississippi—especially those who were part of the existing educational establishment—didn't think that anyone from outside the state should be entrusted with our schools.

But the two of us got along well from the get-go. Over more than three decades working in education, Carey had been a classroom teacher, a principal, an associate superintendent, and then the chief academic officer of the Washington, DC, public school system. She'd spent the majority of her career in Maryland, which ranked first in the nation for five straight years. We thought she was the best candidate we could possibly imagine—passionate and compassionate and ever so competent—and I was proud to lay out some significant political capital to get her appointment approved.

We welcomed Carey to Mississippi in November 2013 and turned the implementation keys over to her with great hope and optimism.

I (Carey) was hopeful and optimistic too. As far as I was concerned, there was nothing wrong with kids in Mississippi. They were just as bright and full of God-given talent as anyone else's kids. They just needed the right strategies in place to help them grow and learn.

But I was also well aware of the size of the challenge.

For one thing, everything I'd heard about the poverty in Mississippi turned out to be something of an understatement. I spent a lot of time traveling around the state in those early days, getting to know the people who had been skeptical that someone from the outside could ever really understand the state's unique opportunities and obstacles. I had a lot of breakfasts, lunches, and dinners with superintendents, teachers, parents, and students. And people were very frank. My chief of staff told me that there were some folks in the state who simply didn't believe that all kids should have an equal chance to succeed—a nod to Mississippi's sad history of racial segregation.

But my commitment was to kids of every race and ethnicity, and in every zip code. I still remember the first time I drove through the Mississippi Delta. There's not much there—you can drive for miles and miles and see nothing but flat land. It's hard to get teachers to go there because, well, when school is over there's not much to do.

And I remember at one meeting, a superintendent stood up and asked me, with a lot of frustration in his voice, "Dr. Wright, how do you expect us to teach these poor kids?" I pride myself on having a good poker face, but inside I was infuriated. *How could you even ask a question like that?* But I composed myself and told this guy that we just had to take control over what we could take control over—which was the school day. We just had to make those hours the best and most impactful they could be for every single kid.

As I traveled around the state, we started to settle on a set of six key goals—six suns around which all our work would orbit. The goals were proficiency growth, high school graduation, early childhood education, professional development for teachers, world-class data systems, and making sure every single school in every single district was meeting a basic bar. If that all doesn't sound terribly revolutionary, consider that Mississippi had never had a goal around early childhood education before, nor had it ever really prioritized teacher professional development.

Working around those six goals, we developed a simple strategic plan and explained—politely!—to everyone at the department that this was going to be how things worked going forward. Not everybody liked it, and not everybody stuck around to help implement it. But that was okay.

One element of our plan that was essential but controversial was that we went out and hired every single literacy coach we could find, putting them through a rigorous interview process to make sure they had the right background knowledge to serve as mentors for our educators. Initially, we assigned these coaches to the schools that had the worst data; I'll never forget one principal telling me he didn't need a coach, to which I responded, "Um, did you look at your numbers?" Teachers loved it, though. And as word began to spread around the state that the coach-supported schools were outperforming those without coaches, soon every school was calling my office, wanting to know when I'd be able to send more coaches.

We were especially focused on making sure every teacher felt supported in teaching the Science of Reading approach. As the governor said, a lot of folks in the education establishment were hesitant to give up on the whole language model. But we brought data to the table and made our case—and we were willing to be tough about it when necessary. For the most part, teachers were persuaded. I remember one breaking down in tears after a training, saying that she felt like she'd failed every child who'd come through her classroom before.

➡➡

Another thing I prioritized was changing the way we communicated with the public about how we were doing. In the beginning, this meant some tough love. Mississippi, like a number of other states, didn't align its testing to the National Assessment of Educational Progress (NAEP) test—so in my first year, our state test reported that more than half of our kids were proficient in reading and math, while the national test had those numbers down at 20 percent.

It's called the "honesty gap," and I wanted to close it right away. We quickly aligned our state standards with the NAEP—and while the results that first year were ugly, the scores soon started to trend in the right direction.

This is where our communications strategy really came into effect. The governor has a saying—"success begets success"—but that's only true if people are *aware* of success when it happens. I designed what I called the A-Tour—a series of media events in every school district to earn an *A* on our rating scale. We'd show up and throw a big party, invite the mayor and the press, and even bring our own videographer to capture content.

The first year, there were nineteen districts that earned an *A* rating. The second year, it was thirty-five. My chief of staff asked me what we were going to do when there were more *A* districts than we had time for on our A-Tour. My reply: "Start earlier." Why wouldn't we want to celebrate all the hard work on the part of students and teachers?

I remember hearing from a member of the community about a barbershop in Jackson where the barbers had created a free, little library—a small nook in the corner of the shop where little ones could come and read while they were waiting for their turns. We loved the story and sent our videographer to film these adorable little vignettes. We even invited the barbers to come to the next state board of education meeting where they could be recognized for their efforts. They all showed up in suits and ties, excited, and we were thrilled to point out that the community could really get involved in a positive way. Once you start looking for bright spots, they appear everywhere.

The two of us quickly developed a really positive relationship. Like a lot of his fellow leaders in Mississippi, Tate comes from the world of business, and so we talked constantly about return on investment. I remember one time, as I was walking him and a group of legislators through a PowerPoint presentation, he stopped me after about the tenth slide. "You've been talking for fifteen minutes now," he said, "and you haven't gotten to the part where you ask us for more money." He was right—I didn't want to just show up with my hand out. I wanted to show that we were achieving the desired outcomes.

I also remember the day in October 2019 when the NAEP scores came out and showed that Mississippi was number one in the nation in reading gains. The lieutenant governor was in Chicago that day, but we spoke on the phone as we were both looking at the front-page news. It deeply touched both of us to see the Magnolia State ranked first in the nation at something to do with education.

It was something of an aha moment for a lot of people. It gave us momentum to keep pushing for change—for example, we got rid of low expectations at the high school level, scheduling more AP-level classes and daring our students to meet the challenge, which they did.

No state improved its fourth-grade reading scores more than Mississippi between 2013, when we ranked forty-ninth in the country, and 2022, when we ranked twenty-first. No state even came close. And nothing makes us prouder than the fact that the gains have accrued to students in all zip codes and of all races and ethnicities. What's more, children of poverty, whether Black, Hispanic, or white, now outperform all their counterparts nationally. Our kids are learning to read faster, reading to learn sooner, and graduating from high school in record numbers.

Our success even survived the crisis of the Covid pandemic and its related learning loss—indeed, the success we'd had prior to the pandemic led to our decision to open schools safely as soon as July of 2020 (by then, Tate had become governor). Knowing how valuable the classroom time was, we weren't willing to resort to remote learning one minute longer than was absolutely necessary.

The whole time, we kept raising our expectations—we hiked the "cut score" for the third-grade reading gate three times—and Mississippi's kids just kept on rising to meet them. We both believe that success begets success, and even though Carey has moved on to run the schools in Maryland (where they're moving forward on similar reforms), we're both confident that Mississippi's "Miracle" is just getting underway.

But fair warning to leaders in other states who want to replicate our success: It won't happen automatically or overnight. It will take a sustained commitment to following the data, an emphasis on continuous improvement, a little bit of patience—and, yes, a fair amount of political will in the face of naysayers.

The truth is, we ran afoul of conventional wisdom more than once along the way, not least when it came to declaring the Science of Reading to be a settled question. Even today, with all the success Mississippi and our fellow Southern states have had in prioritizing phonics, there are those who insist on teaching the whole language approach that we left behind.

Still, behind every decision we made was data. And behind every data point was the face of a child. One part of our accountability model awarded points for the growth of the bottom 25 percent of a school's learners. We used to go to superintendents and ask them if they'd identified the kids in that bottom quartile. If they said yes, we'd ask to see the list. Then we'd point to a single name and ask: *What are you doing for* this *kid, right here?*

Mississippi can now proudly boast that it's doing the very best by all of its kids. And there's no reason other states—red or blue, big or small, rich or poor—can't follow in our footsteps.

5

DELIVERING RESULTS THROUGH THE FINE PRINT

FORMER MAYOR RAHM EMANUEL
(D-CHICAGO)

LISA MORRISON BUTLER, FORMER COMMISSIONER OF THE CHICAGO DEPARTMENT OF FAMILY AND SUPPORT SERVICES

When you're the commissioner of Chicago's Department of Family and Support Services (DFSS), you quickly learn to keep your phone within arm's reach. A big-city mayor's day starts early and ends late. A call could come at any moment. And when a call comes—you answer.

The night we first spoke about expanding the Becoming A Man mentoring program—more commonly referred to as BAM—Lisa had just walked in the door of her condo on a beautiful evening in the late summer of 2016. Suddenly, her phone rang and, glancing at the screen, she saw the three letters that meant the workday still wasn't quite over: MRE.

Mayor Rahm Emanuel.

She picked up on the second ring. "Yes, Mayor."

Rahm, rather famously, isn't one for small talk. "Hey," he said. "I want to expand BAM. Right away."

Within three years, some seven thousand Chicago-area youth had the opportunity to participate in a mentoring program proven effective at reducing crime and improving educational outcomes. Thousands of lives have been changed—and, without a doubt, more than a few have been saved altogether. This success, we firmly believe, is a testament not only to the program itself, but to the power of small levers within government, in this case the humble request for proposals (RFP), to drive meaningful change.

Before we tell the story of how we worked together to scale this impactful mentoring program so it could serve a critical mass of Chicago's young men, it's worth taking a moment to understand where BAM came from and why it's so effective.

The program was the brainchild of a Chicago school psychologist named Anthony Ramirez-Di Vittorio. Back in 2001, "Tony D" (as he was known to his students at Roberto Clemente Community Academy) started taking high school boys out of class for a series of frank but empathetic conversations.

"I started talking to boys about manhood and challenging them to look at themselves," he later told *Forbes*. "I'd listen, empathize, and do men's work: 'You just called this teacher a so-and-so. How did you feel about abusing your teacher? Is that the kind of man you want to be?' I called them on their shit and they loved it and asked for more, and teachers started seeing change and emotional regulation."[1]

As Tony D's conversation circles began to show promise, he gradually formalized the concept, identifying six "core values" around which he could build these conversations: integrity, accountability, self-determination, positive anger expression, respect for womanhood, and goal-setting. A nonprofit called Youth Guidance eventually took over the program and brought it into more schools, where its success continued.

In February 2013, Youth Guidance brought Rahm to a BAM meeting at Harper High School, and the effectiveness of the program was immediately obvious to the mayor. Parts of the program were light and fun—he still remembers badly losing a paper airplane contest—but other parts were deeply emotional, the kind of stuff that sticks with you forever. The young men were willing to be vulnerable—because they felt supported like they'd never been before.

Not long after that session, President Barack Obama came to town and Rahm brought him to another conversation circle, ushering BAM into the national spotlight. That June, a group of BAM students traveled to Washington for an early Father's Day celebration in the East Room of the White House. And when the president launched a mentoring program of his own in 2014—called My Brother's Keeper—he based it in no small part on the work of Youth Guidance and the BAM program.

In 2015, the voters of Chicago re-elected Rahm to a second term. He knew that he wanted to make it a priority to prevent another lost generation of our beloved city's youth. He laid out the challenge in his second inaugural speech, saying, "I have met these young men and women throughout the city. Many of them lack the spark of hope in their eyes that we would never accept in our own children." We both knew that programs like BAM would play a key role in helping the mayor to keep that promise—as he's frequently said, if it were up to him, we'd be assigning mentors to these kids starting in kindergarten.

When it comes to education, the mayor has a specific viewpoint that he often communicates to the rest of us in city government: Our children spend around 20 percent of their time in the classroom. And there's a lot we can do to improve the education they get during those hours. But we spend a lot of time working on education policy, and comparatively little thinking about the other 80 percent. And if you don't get the 80 percent right, it really doesn't matter what goes on in those classrooms—kids born in difficult circumstances don't stand a chance.

That's why we focused so much not just on mentoring programs like BAM, but on other wraparound services like summer jobs, after-school programs, and putting teachers in libraries to serve as tutors.

So we were both already motivated to make mentoring a big piece of the mayor's second-term agenda. But then came the summer of 2016, which brought an unprecedented spasm of gun violence. August alone saw more than four hundred shootings and at least seventy-eight people killed—the deadliest month in decades.[2] We took the crisis not just seriously but *personally*.

The mayor's first call every morning was always with Superintendent of Police Eddie Johnson, which meant that every day began with a grim recitation of the previous night's casualties. The story was almost always the same: one or more young men, lost to the streets.

All summer long, in community meetings, hospital rooms, and funeral homes, Chicagoans shared their anger and anxiety. They expected immediate and meaningful action. And while much of the plan to address the violence would inevitably rely on Superintendent Johnson and the police department, we knew that policing alone would not be enough, and neither would hoping our schools could educate our way out of this mess. We'd have to address the other 80 percent of our children's lives. And that's what led to our fateful conversation on that late summer evening.

➡➡

We're very lucky in Chicago city government to have a unique relationship with the University of Chicago's Urban Labs and its Crime Lab. And in 2015, researchers there published a paper with the National Bureau of Economic Research looking at the BAM model's proven record of success.

The paper, written by a team led by University of Chicago Assistant

Professor of Economics Sara Heller, was entitled "Thinking, Fast and Slow? Some Field Experiments to Reduce Crime and Dropout in Chicago." The title was a reference to a 2011 *New York Times* bestseller by psychologist Daniel Kahneman in which he described two models of thinking that behavioral scientists believe we employ in our daily lives: so-called System 1 thinking that relies almost entirely on instinct, and System 2 thinking that is rooted more in logical analysis. System 1 thinking is fast and automatic and less taxing on our brains, so we tend to use it by default. But it often makes use of mental shortcuts that can affect decision-making, and not always for the better.

According to Heller and her team, System 1 thinking was getting a lot of young men in trouble; their quick reactions to high-pressure situations tended to escalate too often into violence. They theorized that the BAM model was succeeding by teaching them to slow down and use System 2 thinking instead, helping them to avoid those dangerous escalations.

For example: At the time, the first activity in the BAM program involved two students and a ball. One student held the ball, and the other was told that he had thirty seconds to get it from him. In nearly every case, the second student resorted immediately to physical force, attempting to grab the ball. It wasn't until the debrief that the group leader made an observation: *You could have just asked for the ball.*

According to the Crime Lab study, students usually objected, protesting that "he wouldn't have given it" or that "he would have thought I was a punk." But when the group leader turned to the student who was holding the ball he usually rolled his eyes and said something like, "I would have given it; it's just a stupid ball."

Heller and her team hypothesized that "these interventions improve youth outcomes in substantial part because they help youth slow down in high-stakes settings, examine their automatic assumptions about what situation they are in, and ask whether the situation could be construed differently."[3]

That was all interesting—but we're both in the results business, so we were even more excited about the section of the paper illustrating exactly how *well* the model worked: In two trials, one conducted in 2009–10 and the other in 2013–15, Heller's team found that participation in BAM reduced total arrests by a third and violent crime arrests by nearly half. Participants were also likely to be more engaged in their schoolwork and, by nearly 20 percent, more likely to wind up graduating.[4]

(Researchers also experimented with the BAM model at the Cook County Juvenile Temporary Detention Center where they worked with high-risk juvenile arrestees. They found that going through the BAM program reduced recidivism rates by 21 percent.)[5]

We're both big data nerds to begin with—and when the mayor is out talking to potential funding partners, he always likes to have evidence like this in his pocket. He always says that these potential funders—with a million different claims on their time, energy, and money—are trying to cover a huge present with a tiny square of wrapping paper. The way you stand out is by showing them the real-world potential impact of their investment. And just as there's nothing like hard data when you're trying to solve a problem, there's nothing like it when you're trying to convince people that you've got the right solution in hand.

The two of us played very different roles in city government. And while Rahm was out there leading the public-facing charge for more mentoring—and raising money to make it possible—Lisa and the team at DFSS were getting to work thinking about how to implement the initiative.

Before coming to DFSS, Lisa had served as the head of the education nonprofit City Year Chicago. When she went into schools, she frequently encountered BAM counselors in their black T-shirts. So she was just as excited as the mayor was. But she also recognized that he had placed an imposing challenge in front of her.

The truth was, no matter how much money we directed Youth Guidance's way, relying on BAM itself to cover every at-risk student in the city simply wouldn't be programmatically feasible—to say nothing of the fact that it wouldn't be fair to other organizations that might want to be part of the solution.

To get us started, we asked the University of Chicago's Education Lab—a sister of the Crime Lab—to help us figure out exactly who our target population for mentoring should be. They leapt into action, quickly identifying a group of 7,200 young men, each enrolled in eighth, ninth, or tenth grade in a Chicago public school and each living or attending school in one of twenty-two specific at-risk neighborhoods. It was extremely helpful work, but it only served to underline the challenge of scaling up existing programming—at the time, DFSS was funding only around eight hundred mentoring slots, and those were scattered across a variety of organizations, each with their own approach to the project.

So we had a big challenge on our hands—and we were driving at a hard deadline: The mayor had a big speech scheduled for the end of September where he wanted to go public with a comprehensive plan, which included the hiring of nearly a thousand additional police officers, policy reforms to help them combat crime, and the launch of what would come to be known as the Mayor's Mentoring Initiative, or MMI.

That day, his voice cracked as he described the impact of the summer's violence: "I see kids today, a look in their eyes where the vitality, the hope, and the purpose has been stolen from them because of the harshness of this city. It has been robbed from them. And we cannot avert our eyes as a city any longer." Thanks in no small part to the Crime Lab's research, the mayor was also able to tell Chicagoans that, while the city would cover half of the $36 million cost over the next three years, the rest would come from corporations like Exelon and Peoples Gas, as well as from individuals like Jimmy Liautaud, the owner and founder of the sandwich chain Jimmy John's.

The first step, we decided, would be to expand the BAM program itself as far as we could. Two weeks after Rahm delivered that big speech, we announced new funding that would help Youth Guidance bring the BAM model to an additional 1,300 students in the 2016–17 school year. "Important investments in mentoring that have the power to turn young people's lives around cannot wait for the next budget season," the mayor said in a press release—and you'd better believe we cited all that evidence yet again.

But we wanted to serve 7,200 kids, which meant we had to find several thousand more mentoring slots. In order to do that, we'd need to find new partners. And the clock was ticking. Every morning, the mayor would talk with Police Superintendent Johnson and feel the pressure to act—pressure he passed on to the rest of the team. To fulfill the promise of MMI, we would need to scale the BAM model at great speed. Ironically, however, our first step would be to slow down.

Lisa had been at DFSS for about a year when this all started, inheriting a really well-run department with a strong reputation and a healthy budget. But government can have its own particular inertia, and the status quo can be difficult to shake. Coming in the door, she had made it a priority to connect one-on-one with as many of her staff as possible, listening to them and learning from them. Over and over, she asked the same five questions: *What's the biggest opportunity we face right now? What would we have to do to realize it? What's the biggest threat we face? Why are we facing it? If you were me, what would you do right now?*

The conversations were illuminating not just because of how DFSS staffers answered those questions, but because of the question so many of them asked in return: *Is every dollar we spend working as hard as it should?* Like many social service agencies, DFSS took in a lot of money from the federal and state governments—and, like many social service agencies, DFSS spent a lot of time answering for all that funding. The staff was constantly responding to inquiries and fielding clarifying questions from those who were higher up in the funding stream, leaving little bandwidth to help the nonprofits that received DFSS funding spend it effectively. "We had become," Lisa later told the Harvard Kennedy School Government Performance Lab (GPL), "really good box checkers."[6] But the team at DFSS wanted to do more—to *be* more.

Soon, we began to prioritize procurement as a core element of DFSS's strategy, explaining to the team that the department would take a more results-oriented, data-driven approach to funding projects in the city. And at the heart of this shift would be the way DFSS began to treat one crucial step of that process: the RFP.

Before Lisa's arrival, requests for proposals were considered quotidian administrative tasks—a burden, really, usually delegated to staff that were lower in the pecking order. Leadership rarely engaged with the RFP process at all, and if they did, it was usually only to quickly approve a draft. In fact, in many cases, today's RFP would just be a copy of yesterday's—hauled out of storage and with a new date slapped over the old one. And once the money was in the field, there was little chance to engage with funding recipients. It wouldn't be until the contract was up that DFSS could examine what had gone well and what could have gone better. This felt like a big missed opportunity.

Sitting with the mayor's urgent demand for action, Lisa knew that the traditional approach of releasing a cursory RFP was not the right way to ensure success, even though doing so would allow money to move into the field as quickly and effortlessly as possible. This time had to be different. This time, DFSS would dedicate time in the funding process to gather information and ask questions. With so much research at hand from the Crime Lab and others, the Youth Services Division team would produce a more detailed, more thoughtful RFP—and, hopefully, receive more effective proposals.

This isn't to say the mayor wasn't impatient. Commissioners like Lisa had to submit weekly reports every Friday detailing exactly how much progress they'd achieved that week. The mayor, in turn, would spend the weekend with these reports, handing them back on Monday morning marked up with questions and new ideas. We were both invested in getting this done as quickly as possible.

But we also had a level of trust built up such that the team was allowed to do its job. In short order, we identified three outcome areas—three definitions of success: achieving positive school outcomes, lowering involvement in the justice system, and connecting participants to appropriate employment opportunities.

We also leaned on the Crime Lab's examination of the BAM program to develop a set of best practices for mentoring that potential grantees would have to employ:

1. Sustained contact. Youth and caring adults have at least five hours of contact per month.
2. Group/cohort participation. Youth participate in a cohort during the program and become an important support system for each other.
3. Skill development and training. Mentors use a set curriculum as well as experiential learning to help youth grow and develop new skills.
4. Socio-emotional needs. Programs provide the support and resources necessary for youth to grow socially and emotionally.
5. Positive setting. Programs incorporate positive values, principles, and practices.

It took until December for the new RFP to be ready. Unlike many previous RFPs, this one clearly identified both the focal population and the desired outcomes, and it specified *how* those outcomes were to be achieved: through those five research-backed best practices.

The process of applying would also be different. Even before entering a bid, organizations wishing to participate in the initiative would first have to demonstrate their presence in a targeted neighborhood, their experience in successfully mentoring young men, and their capacity to expand. Only by proving that they met these baseline qualifications would they earn the chance to submit proposals that would then be graded against a scorecard that mirrored the RFP—a novel, if commonsense, step that avoided any surprises in the selection process.

This new process asked a lot more of potential grantees—and a lot more of the DFSS staff tasked with interfacing with those applicants. Changing how things worked risked creating friction between the department and its nonprofit partners, and it was up to people like Monica Dunleavy-Gerster, the agency's youth services coordinator, to keep things running smoothly.

"It wasn't easy for our unit," Monica said. "Smaller and medium organizations loved the idea that we were going to serve all these boys, but we had to get buy-in."[7] This proved tricky in an arena where many organizations had long-established practices DFSS was looking to change to align with the research. Some organizations argued that the initiative should include a broader age range, and others believed that it should include young women as well as men. And while this feedback would be incorporated into later iterations of the mentoring RFP, for now, DFSS staff like Monica had to hold the line. The message from the city had to be clear and consistent: *We have the research on our side—and now our job is to help you incorporate this set of best practices into what you're already doing.*

Even after being selected for funding, the process wouldn't be over. We established "learning cohorts"—regular sessions over the course of the initial funding year in which nonprofits would come together to review and share data. If an agency was having trouble recruiting mentors or struggling to incorporate a particular component of the best practices, it could bring the issue to the cohort and get support from DFSS and other grantees working on the same problems.

No longer would DFSS have to wait until the end of a contract to find out whether it had been effective. Now that conversation would take place on a quarterly basis throughout the first year of the contract. And instead of merely monitoring for contract compliance, DFSS staff like Monica Dunleavy-Gerster could spend their time supporting grantees in their quest to achieve the outcomes specified in the RFP, serving as full partners rather than simply checking boxes.

Despite the more deliberate RFP process, money quickly began to flow into the field. In March 2017, we were able to announce that forty-six community-based organizations had received contracts, adding another 1,200 mentoring slots and putting the city more than 60 percent toward its goal of serving 7,200 young men. And in October 2018, we announced an increase in city funding to serve another 600 seventh graders.

Meanwhile, DFSS enlisted the University of Chicago's Education Lab once again, this time to conduct a study on whether MMI was reaching its target population.

The results were encouraging: More than 5,800 young men had been successfully enrolled in mentoring programs, and 99 percent of them were living or going to school in one of the twenty-two high-risk neighborhoods the team had previously identified. Compared to young men of similar ages attending Chicago public schools, those in a program were more than twice as likely to have experienced homelessness or a temporary living situation, 2.3 times more likely to have had at least one arrest, and 2.4 times more likely to have been the victim of a crime.

The study also showed that more than half of the young men spent more than five months in mentoring programs, with participants receiving an average of three hours of group mentoring and one hour of one-on-one mentoring each month—these numbers went up during the summer months.[8]

Later, the researchers turned their attention to surveying participants about their experiences in the program. Again, the results were overwhelmingly positive: More than 80 percent of participants reported strong relationships in their mentoring programs and more than 70 percent reported strong levels of social-emotional competencies. We celebrated these results—and then immediately turned around and incorporated them into the RFP process, creating a set of performance indicators for grantees based on these metrics.

It's now been almost a decade since we worked together to create the Mayor's Mentoring Initiative, and while neither of us is still working in city government, we're proud that the mentoring initiative endures—and that thousands of young men have had the opportunity to benefit from city-funded mentorship programs that used research-tested best practices.

But to be clear, credit doesn't belong to city leaders alone—far from it. Indeed, we would point to three key ingredients that enabled this success story: ingredients other cities would need to replicate our success.

First, and perhaps most importantly, we had a department staff committed to the project. Instead of insisting on doing things "the way they've always been done," DFSS employees like Monica

Dunleavy-Gerster understood that the old approach of cranking out carbon-copy RFPs was outdated. They were willing to do the "prework" of gathering data and identifying best practices in order to develop a more dynamic RFP that would lead to more data-driven policymaking and, ultimately, better outcomes.

Second, we had a philanthropic community eager to pitch in. The mayor used the city's initial financial commitment to make the case that private and social sector support was critical—and that it would be effective. That said, while philanthropic support was key to quickly expanding evidence-based mentoring practices throughout the city, partner organizations note that the private funding landscape is always changing. In recent years, the initiative has largely been funded with city dollars.

Third, and deeply relevant to this book: We had really good data. Not only did the department have randomized controlled trials on a local mentorship program to inform its RFP, but it also had data on the youth it wanted to reach through its partnership with the University of Chicago and its Urban Labs. Data collection did not end with the issuance of the RFP, either. DFSS staff and Urban Labs worked with grantees to collect and analyze data throughout the life of the contract and to use that data to help inform future RFPs.

We're proud of the way we used data in expanding mentoring in Chicago. We're proud of the way city staff stepped up, finding pressure points in the fine print of governance and using them to drive real results. And we're especially proud of the results showing a decrease in violent crime after we implemented the mayor's initiative. But, as always, the most rewarding part of the work isn't found in the numbers, but rather in the human stories.

Rahm, in particular, will never forget meeting a young man named Marcus Norris at that very first BAM meeting back in 2013. When Marcus was nine years old, a stray bullet crashed through the window of his house in Chicago and knocked out four of his teeth. For years, he went through life too embarrassed to smile—but he never told anyone why.

It wasn't until he joined BAM that he began to let his guard down. It didn't happen right away—his mentor, Timothy Jackson, has said that he almost kicked Marcus out of the group for goofing off—but after several weeks of regular meetings, Marcus finally told his story. And as he began to confide in his mentor, Marcus began to grow more and more confident, imagining some big things for himself.

"I got shot before," he said the day Rahm visited, "and I could have died or went the wrong route, but this program brought me to my senses, and I stay in school and do good." Indeed, at a school where almost a third of the seniors didn't graduate in 2014, Marcus put himself on a path not only to finish high school, but to go off to college and become a chef—his dream.

That's not all. At Timothy's urging, Youth Guidance launched a fundraiser to pay for Marcus to have his teeth fixed. So not only did Marcus get to take a graduation photo—in it, he's wearing a huge smile. How can you beat a story like that?

6

BRIDGES OUT OF POVERTY IN RURAL AMERICA

COMMISSIONER LESLIE MEYER
(R-AUDRAIN COUNTY, MISSOURI)

Mexico, Missouri: the seat of Audrain County and the fire-brick capital of the world.

At least, it was when I moved to this small city in central Missouri in 1999 to take a reporting job at *The Mexico Ledger*. At its peak, the A. P. Green plant kept about two thousand people in steady work building fire-resistant bricks that lined the kilns of steel plants across America and even the NASA rocket-launch site at Cape Canaveral. That refractory was the beating heart of Mexico.[1]

And then, it wasn't. Within a year of my arrival, the plant began to lay people off, and by 2002, it had closed its doors for good. It was the kind of loss that can destroy a rural community. But not Mexico. We pivoted—to manufacturing car parts, to ethanol and biodiesel plants, to farming. Today, Audrain County's population stands strong at around twenty-five thousand people. Most folks from outside Missouri probably couldn't place us on a map, but we have a diverse and thriving business community.[2]

In time, I pivoted too. I went from print reporting to radio advertising, wound up starting my own small business, and, eventually, won a seat on the three-member Audrain County Commission, where I've served since 2021.

They say rural America is in steep decline. Places like Mexico, left behind by globalization and automation, are supposed to be in an economic doom loop, spiraling into poverty and blight. But that's not our reality. In the real Mexico, Missouri, we're building a stronger economy—and a stronger *community* too.

Doing so has taken the enthusiastic and generous participation of not just elected officials like me, but also civic leaders at the chamber of commerce, farsighted business owners who embrace their role as community leaders, and a resilient workforce willing to do what it takes to overcome obstacles to opportunity. Mexico is proving that we have what it takes to meet the demands of the twenty-first-century economy—and that, even in the forgotten places in our country, there is room for ordinary people to achieve the American Dream.

There's no doubt that rural leaders like me face different challenges than the big-city mayors featured throughout this book. But we've proven that the leadership formula that works for them works for us too. As a community, we identified proven strategies to address a problem we were facing and made the necessary investments so that these strategies could make a meaningful difference. Indeed, you might be surprised to learn just how small of an investment it can take to matter—and how big a difference doing what works can make for a community like ours.

If you want to understand what makes Mexico strong, you have to meet Dana Keller. She's been the executive director of our chamber of commerce since 2009, and she's an essential figure in Mexico's success story—the kind of person who knows how to bring people together and lead them forward.

A little over a decade ago, Mexico Public Schools connected with an organization called Bright Futures, which brings together schools and the business community to provide wraparound services for kids.

We have great teachers and administrators in Audrain County, but many of our kids grow up poor, and it's not uncommon to see students arrive at school without appropriate clothing or anything in their lunch boxes. Following the Bright Futures model, Dana brought business leaders into the schools for a program called Lunch Buddies. There was no formal agenda—just business executives dropping by to have lunch with kids.

For students, these informal lunch sessions were invaluable opportunities to receive mentoring. One school nurse told Dana that she used to have a group of kids she called "frequent fliers"—they weren't sickly, but they wound up in the nurse's office multiple times a week just because they craved attention from a responsible adult. Once Lunch Buddies got started, that stopped.

Meanwhile, for the business leaders, it was a chance to see clearly exactly how much extra support kids and families in our region really needed—a much-needed wakeup call.

It was through this program that Dana became acquainted with the work of Dr. Ruby Payne, an educator and author who has written extensively about the culture of poverty. Her first book, *A Framework for Understanding Poverty*, sold more than a million copies, launched thousands of workshops, and changed the national conversation about the realities of life for the working poor. People in poverty, she argued, live by different, "hidden" rules that govern everything from the way they communicate to the way they learn. And if we don't understand those rules, we can't hope to connect with poor kids, help them work their way into the middle class, and break the cycle of generational poverty.[3]

In 1999, Dr. Payne published another book called *Bridges Out of Poverty*, aimed at bringing the same lessons she'd taught educators to professionals in social, legal, and health services. People living in poverty, for example, are more driven by the need to maintain the family and social relationships that help keep them afloat. Their image of power comes less from their expertise or their connections and more from the amount of respect they're able to garner in the people they meet. They budget differently, dream differently, even speak differently. And while no one should underestimate the resourcefulness of people struggling just to get by, we also shouldn't confuse the skills that are necessary for survival with the ones that are necessary for getting ahead.[4]

Dr. Payne's book was passed around the chamber of commerce's offices, with a copy making its way to us on the county commission. One local business owner, who claimed he hadn't finished a book since high school, took a copy to his deer stand in the winter and read it. Then, in 2017, Dana Keller brought a delegation, including my colleague Commissioner Tracy Graham, to Atlanta for a "Building Bridges Out of Poverty" conference sponsored by Dr. Payne's organization.

They were there in the hopes of better understanding a phenomenon that was posing an urgent threat to our community's economic future: the seeming inability of our local businesses to keep workers on the job.

To be clear, this wasn't the kind of workforce *development* challenge you've read about elsewhere in this book. This was about workforce *retention*. Qualified employees—people who needed these jobs to stay afloat—were quitting in droves. One business in town lost eighty-five workers in a single year. And this was posing a huge problem for the bottom lines of our businesses. Dana did a little math and discovered that, when you added up the time and effort it took to find and train a new worker, each position turned over could cost an employer anywhere from $2,500 to as much as $5,500. We needed to find out why this was happening.

In Atlanta, our delegation got some answers. It's not hard to imagine how being poor might make it hard to find a job—how, after all, are you supposed to get to work if you can't afford transportation or childcare or a uniform? But the conference opened our eyes to the reality that living in poverty can make it hard to *keep* a job for many of the same reasons. For example: If you're the only person in a relative's life who has a car, and that relative has a medical appointment, you're going to skip work to bring him or her to the doctor, even if doing so risks your continued employment. Our workers, we realized, weren't quitting because they didn't like their jobs. They were quitting because their lives outside work were making their jobs impossible to do.

When our delegation got back home, we all put our heads together and developed an initiative focused on dealing with these challenges called the Mexico Sustainability Project (MSP). And in 2021, we took advantage of a small regional grant from the Mark Twain Regional Council of Governments and launched the Workforce Resource Assistance Program (WRAP) with one simple idea in mind: Life doesn't stop when the workday begins, and when personal challenges make it hard to get to work, stay at work, or do your best at work, there should be someone *at* work who cares enough to help.

When we set out to design WRAP, we looked at some prepackaged programs made available by for-profit companies and quickly realized we couldn't afford them. We would need to figure out our own path forward. With help from organizations like the United Way, we pulled together a set of procedures and made an offer to area employers: If you have 150 employees or fewer, we'll put a workforce retention specialist in your building for three hours a week—plus your employees will have 24/7 access to our programming—for the low price of $7,500 a year. If you're a bigger company, we'll ask you to chip in $10,000.

It was the deal of the century for local businesses. If taking advantage of WRAP kept just a couple of employees from quitting over an issue that would have been manageable, they'd come out ahead.

WRAP started with buy-in from four of Mexico's biggest employers—Fluid Power Support, Gold Crest Distributing, True Manufacturing, and Spartan Light Metal Products—and one dynamic workforce retention specialist named Darlene Shopher.

Darlene's the other person you have to know in order to understand this success story. Dana pulled her out of retirement after a career that included more than a decade working in the mental health system in various roles and then more than twenty years working as a counselor in a middle school. There isn't much Darlene hasn't seen—which made her the perfect person to spend her week on shop floors, listening to employees talk about what's going on in their lives and connecting them with the solutions they're searching for.

That last part is important. Darlene isn't just there as a friendly ear or a shoulder to cry on. She's a problem-solver. And she's got some incredible stories to share about the work she's been able to do with WRAP.

One day, for example, a guy in his sixties showed up to her office hours on a factory floor. He was a good, solid worker who'd been at the company for a long time—not the kind of guy who asks for help easily—but he'd gotten himself into a bit of a financial fix. He and his wife couldn't see eye to eye on the family budget, and he'd wound up unable to pay his property taxes. Darlene empathized with his situation—and then got to work helping to resolve it. In the end, he was able to open a Christmas account at a separate bank where the money would be guaranteed not to be spent until the end of the year when taxes were due.

This particular gentleman was fortunate enough that a simple bit of accounting helped to solve his problem. Many others, however, run into financial dilemmas that aren't so easily solved. Dana estimates that 70 percent of the people in town can't handle a $400 emergency. And, in Missouri, lots of folks who run into money trouble resort to payday loans. In our state, for whatever reason, these predatory lenders are allowed to charge outrageous interest rates. It's not at all uncommon to run into someone who's got a loan with a 250 percent rate. It's the kind of "solution" that winds up being a bigger, totally unmanageable problem. People lose their cars, their homes, their chance at digging out of the hole. It's just another way it's expensive to be poor.

That's why WRAP went to a couple of local financial institutions and raised a small pool of money to be loaned out in case of emergency. The way it works is that you see Darlene and get the 800 bucks you need to fix your roof or whatever, and the amount you owe is automatically taken out of your paycheck every pay period—not at a usurious 250 percent interest rate but at a dramatically lower fair-market rate. Here's the best part: Typically, even after they've paid back the loan, people tend to keep having that small deduction taken out of their checks and diverted into a savings account. That way, not only do they get past the emergency without signing up for a payday loan, they get to start building a nest egg of their very own—not to mention getting a boost to their credit rating. Dana estimates that this program alone has saved Mexico workers a quarter of a million dollars over the past four years[5]—that's real money that, instead of going to some shifty payday lender, stayed right here in our community.

Financial literacy is a big deal to people teetering on the edge of poverty—so we created a financial-wellness program consisting of monthly in-person education classes at jobsites, access to a financial coach with support via phone and email, and an online platform people can access anytime.

Darlene spends a lot of time helping people figure out money. But her job isn't just about dollars and cents. WRAP has an emotional-wellness program where people can come learn more about things like managing stress, beating addiction, and communicating effectively with loved ones. Darlene likes to tell the story of one company where the housekeeping staff that cleaned the offices at night observed that the grounds were cleaner than they used to be, and folks seemed more calm—the result of six months in the WRAP program.

The best part is that workers aren't just allowed to take an hour off work to attend one of these workshops—they're actively encouraged. Their bosses understand that financial stability and emotional wellness are essential in retaining their workforce, and they're eager to see people take advantage of WRAP's services. The floor manager at one company even *requires* employees to visit with Darlene regularly. "I don't care if you talk about the weather," he told his crew, "but you've got to know who she is so that if you ever need her, she can be there for you."

And while you might think some employers would recoil at the notion that their employees don't feel adequately supported, the truth is that most really do want what's best for their workforce. At one jobsite there was a lot of food insecurity, which of course the bosses had no idea about. But when employees mentioned it to Darlene, the company set out a spread of oatmeal and granola bars and fruit in the break room—within a couple of months, that issue had been resolved.

I'll give you one more example, and this one I really love because it involves the whole community. One reason people often miss work is to go to court—for a summons, for a child support or custody hearing, or to testify in a domestic violence case. Often, folks will be told to show up at eight in the morning for a hearing that doesn't actually take place until three in the afternoon. It's a long day of waiting—and not getting paid. We went to the courts and asked if they'd be willing to send people off with notes they could use to explain their daylong absences from work. They told us they could do us one better—if someone at one of our jobsites had a court appointment, they'd move it to the front of the docket so they could get back to work faster.

WRAP has been an unqualified success for Mexico. One company went from 40 percent turnover to 5 percent in just a few years, saving millions—and more and more businesses are signing on each year. Darlene even had to hire a couple more workforce retention specialists (although she still manages to be seemingly everywhere all the time).

And recently, we got a grant from the National Association of Counties's Rural Leaders for Economic Mobility program to offer training for employers across central Missouri who want to follow in Mexico's footsteps. We were proud to host a cohort of local leaders from rural communities across the country right here in Audrain

County, where they got to meet with folks like Dana and Darlene and bring home with them not just their stories, but their guidance on how to create successes of their own.

➡➡

I grew up in a very rural community on the banks of the Mississippi River. I've seen what it looks like when a small town dies—when a vibrant downtown starts to dry up, the jobs move away, and people settle into a life of low expectations and limited opportunity.

That's not going to happen to Mexico. In Mexico, we've built a community where we look out for each other, a community where businesses take an active interest in lifting up their workers, a community where everyone pitches in and everyone gets a chance. We may not be the fire-brick capital of the world anymore, but we are still home to the Miss Missouri pageant—and, more importantly, we've become an example of what is possible when you make smart, targeted investments in programs you know to be effective.

You'll notice one thing missing from this story: a big infusion of government money. With WRAP, we have built a lean homegrown program powered by big-hearted locals like Dana and Darlene, and sustained by a business community that is fully invested in its success. But that doesn't mean there's no role for government to play. Our county commission, including our Presiding Commissioner Alan Winders, has championed the program, helped enlist more local partners, and worked to expand it to serve even more residents. If other places made small seed investments like we were able to do here in Audrain County, they'd see the same kind of buy-in from the business community—and, in a short time, the same kind of results we've been able to achieve. Frankly, it's the kind of program that, if the money were available, should exist everywhere.

The model is there. The data is there. The results are there. And I'm here to tell you that, by helping your workforce build bridges out of poverty, your community, too, can build a bridge to a brighter economic future.

7

GOOD IDEAS TRAVEL

MAYOR RANDALL WOODFIN
(D-BIRMINGHAM)

Here are two numbers you should know if you care about kids.

First: 90 percent of a child's brain development occurs before the age of five.[1]

Second: Research shows that, in order to maximize that development, a child under the age of five should hear at least twenty-one thousand words every single day.[2]

As the father of two young children myself, I know that parents worry about everything. Are we feeding our kids right? Should I have packed a sweater for the playground? How much screen time is too much? But it turns out that, if you want your children to succeed, you can go a long way just by giving them the gift of words. It doesn't matter if you're reading a book or singing a song or just chatting about your day—every word a child hears literally grows his or her brain.

We know from research—and you've read in this book—that you can draw a straight line backward from economic mobility to education and that, even within the education system, the line goes back from postsecondary credentials to high school graduation to middle-grade reading and math basics to kindergarten readiness. And, in fact, it stretches back even farther than that. It's not an exaggeration to say that talking to your kids when they're still in diapers is one of the best ways to set them up for economic success as an adult.

But not every child is equally likely to reach that magic number of twenty-one thousand words a day. As you might suspect, kids in families higher up on the socioeconomic spectrum tend to hear far more words than those who start in families with fewer opportunities. This "word gap" can be as big as 30 million by the age of four.[3] So if you're the mayor of a big city where too many kids are falling behind before they even get a fair shot, and you want to improve economic mobility for low-income families, closing that word gap is a great place to start.

This leads me to a third research-backed number I'll never forget: High-quality investments in early childhood education can deliver a 13 percent annual return on investment.[4]

I'm the mayor of Birmingham, Alabama, a city where, when I took office, only 17 percent of our third graders were proficient in reading. This chapter tells the story of how we made improving early childhood education—specifically, closing the word gap—first a priority and ultimately a reality. Participants in the program we launched are three times more likely to be ready for kindergarten—and both families and childcare providers report that they're reading more and enjoying it. It's a true success story.

It's also a story of how good ideas spread. This story starts years before I was sworn in as mayor. And it starts about 1,100 miles away, in the city of Providence, Rhode Island.

In 2013, Bloomberg Philanthropies held its inaugural Mayors Challenge. Cities from around the world were invited to enter, each pitching a new idea that would solve a major challenge they were facing. Winners would receive not just millions in financial support from the foundation, but also logistical and staff support to help get the idea up on its feet.

Under the leadership of then-Mayor Angel Taveras, Providence won the grand prize with one commonsense idea: *Let's help lower-income parents and other caregivers talk more with kids at the earliest possible stage.*

It was a simple idea whose execution relied on a simple piece of technology: a small hunk of gray and purple plastic the size of a pager manufactured by a Colorado nonprofit called LENA. Inside is a tiny digital language recorder, and the whole thing slips into a vest worn by a young child. The device stays on all day, measuring how many words adults speak near the child, as well as how many back-and-forth exchanges, or "conversational turns," the child has with an adult.

In other words, it's a "word pedometer." And the system as a whole works exactly the way using a Fitbit or other pedometer works for someone who wants to exercise more: A small, unobtrusive device gives you data to track how you're doing, which encourages you to do better. Providence used the $5 million grant from Bloomberg Philanthropies to equip participating families with a LENA recorder, as well as coaching from language development professionals who used the data from the recorders to provide customized reports—and, critically, positive reinforcement. All of this came at no charge to families.

The new initiative was dubbed Providence Talks, and a 2014 pilot enrolled more than 170 families. The results were clear and unambiguous:

- More than half of the children who enrolled started the program hearing far fewer than the twenty-one thousand words per day necessary for healthy brain development. In fact, the average was closer to eight thousand words per day.
- Families who completed four or more coaching sessions increased the number of words spoken in the home by an average of 1,191 words—and for families who started in the

bottom half of the group, the increase was even larger (4,222 more words on average).

- Importantly, parents *loved* it. Survey respondents reported an overall satisfaction rate of 97 percent.[5] (Take it from a mayor—you usually can't get 97 percent of people to agree on Free Ice Cream Day.)

Encouraged by these results, Providence Talks expanded to reach thousands more children, not just in homes but in day care centers as well. And over the next three years, researchers at Brown University confirmed that the program was helping to stimulate more brain-building conversations for kids, effectively working to close the "word gap."

That's why, in 2018, Bloomberg Philanthropies decided to replicate the program across the country, opening up an opportunity for cities to apply for funding through its What Works Cities initiative.

When I was first elected mayor of my hometown back in 2017, I entered city hall on a mission: invest in our children at every stage of their development. I knew from my time on the school board that securing our city's future meant supporting the young people who would inherit it.

And while I frequently used that "13 percent annual return on investment" number when arguing for more investments in early childhood education in particular, I didn't need to see hard data to understand the importance of those investments. Back before I ran for mayor, I did a TED Talk where I compared early childhood education to the foundation of a home. For all the money we spend in this country on education, I argued, we tend to ignore those first critical years before school even begins, spending only 4 percent of education-focused philanthropy on the early years of a child's development. And no matter how much you spend on the walls, windows, and roof, without a strong foundation the house is eventually going to crumble.

That's exactly what was happening in Alabama, where we don't spend money on a per-pupil basis until our kids get to kindergarten.

Mayors enter office with a sense of urgency and possibility, buoyed by the mandate they've received from voters. But I didn't feel like I had time to take the city down untested pathways. And I didn't have the luxury of living within a "Birmingham bubble." I needed to take the best, most proven ideas and be willing to implement them swiftly.

So if you're wondering whether it bothered me, this idea of borrowing an idea from another city, the answer is: absolutely not. Quite the opposite, really. Here we had a chance to move into a furnished apartment of a policy idea, one that had already been tested, refined, and proven effective.

In partnership with The Overton Project (a social impact incubator founded by Birmingham native Jared Weinstein), we eagerly applied to the program and were honored to be selected as one of five cities to receive funding from Bloomberg Philanthropies to launch our own version of Providence Talks.

That wasn't the end of the story, though. In fact, it was just the beginning of the work.

We couldn't just slap the word "Birmingham" over the word "Providence" and call it a day. As James Anderson, who leads the Government

Innovation program at Bloomberg Philanthropies, has written, cities love to borrow from other cities. But it's not that simple, as Anderson wrote in 2024:

> Cities struggle to convert that interest into results; the path to successfully adopting an idea that's worked elsewhere is fraught with obstacles. First, local governments must find workable ideas at the time they need them—a needle in the haystack challenge. They then must determine how to apply a new strategy to their local and cultural circumstances. Ideas also need to be compelling to potential funders, residents, and existing system stakeholders—people and organizations often vested in maintaining the failed or underperforming status quo. Municipal leaders must overcome these hurdles with little reliable data about what made an intervention effective elsewhere, and without the capacity needed to develop the plans, secure the financing, and build the partnerships essential to see an idea to fruition. Those are challenges that can stop change in its tracks.[6]

Our challenge, then, wasn't just finding the idea, or even convincing Bloomberg to fund our effort at duplicating Providence's success. It was figuring out how to adapt what worked so well in Rhode Island for our city in Alabama. And that's where a pivotal figure enters the story: a woman by the name of Ruth Ann Moss.

The first time I met Ruth Ann—this is how she tells the story, anyway—I was on my knees in the hallway of an elementary school, having a very important conversation with a fourth grader (probably about Pokémon or something). At the time, I was still school board president, and Ruth Ann was struck by the fact that I was actually talking to kids in a school. It was because of that chance meeting that she trusted in me, and a great relationship was born.

Ruth Ann started her career as a Teach for America corps member, and after four years in the classroom she joined the staff of the organization in Alabama to support and develop early-career teachers. She was great at it, consistently being ranked in the top ten coaches in the country. And she was the perfect choice to lead what, at the time, we called Birmingham Talks (we later renamed it Small Magic).

In addition to bringing on Ruth Ann, we made some important early decisions.

For one thing, we decided—unlike most of the other cities that received funding from Bloomberg—not to have the program live inside of city hall. Believe me, it wasn't because I didn't have a personal stake in its success. In fact, it was precisely because I cared so much about Birmingham Talks succeeding that we decided to set it up outside of the apparatus of government.

I'm a proud progressive, but I agree with some conservatives that government should specialize in doing the things it's good at. City hall is really good at managing a lot of things—waste management, police response, infrastructure—but when it comes to education, I think we need to empower people who actually know what they're doing and then get government largely out of the way. I also wanted the program to get set up quickly and for the long haul—two things government often has trouble accomplishing.

Make no mistake: We were all-in on this idea. But we wanted it to *work*—and, to my mind, that meant trusting the Birmingham Talks team to lead.

As they planned for the program's launch, the team held focus groups to get a sense of what parents and caregivers in the city would best respond to. They were surprised by some of the findings. For example—and maybe this is a thought you've had after reading about LENA's technology—Ruth Ann and her team were ready to allay concerns about privacy, explaining that none of what the "word pedometers" heard would be recorded or even heard by anyone else. But parents weren't as concerned about that. Instead, the technology excited them. And when Ruth Ann and the team floated gift cards as incentives for participating, parents told them that they preferred books and other educational items.

In other words, we made a lot of tweaks to the Providence Talks model before we went live with a pilot of Birmingham Talks in 2019.

Bloomberg's investment ran for three years—which meant we had three years to establish proof of concept before we'd need to raise money to fill the gap. And even though we started small, we quickly began to ramp up the program. In 2020 (despite the pandemic), we served 93 kids and two childcare centers. In 2021, it was 539 kids and eleven childcare centers. In our third year, 2022, it was 665 kids and thirteen childcare centers.

That year, I went to the city council and asked for a seven-figure municipal investment to support the work of Birmingham Talks—effectively doubling the Bloomberg funding. They agreed. And the next year, 2023, we were able to double the size of our program team and expand our services to over 900 kids and twenty-one childcare centers. We're now on track to serve more than 1,600 kids a year—and that number is only going to grow.

Our research indicates that 58 percent of childcare providers and 75 percent of families who participate in the program are reading to kids more often as a result. And we're looking forward to seeing proof of this borne out as these kids grow up and hit literacy checkpoints they might not have otherwise hit—the first generation of kids to benefit from the program will be taking their third-grade literacy tests in the 2027–28 school year.

But what really puts a smile on my face is another number: 91 percent of childcare providers who participated in the program told us that it made a positive impact on their classroom. And 84 percent of families said they enjoy spending time with their kids more, as a result of participating.

Last year, a reporter for AL.com interviewed some of the families participating in the program. One mom, Amber Martin, told the paper that she spends all day talking to her five-month-old son. She raved about "being able to start that learning at home and be the ones that set that foundation for him to say education doesn't have to be difficult or hard. It doesn't have to be something that scares you or you're fearful of. It could absolutely be something that piques your curiosity, that you love, that you enjoy doing."

Another parent, Patrile Stallworth, said the program made her three-year-old daughter more engaged. "I felt proud to see it happen right before our eyes. Watching them having an aha moment, or a light bulb going off, or them using words that you didn't know they knew the definition of no matter how big or small the word is, it's just fascinating," she said, adding, "It's just very rewarding as a parent to be able to have those small moments of validation."[7]

It's pretty darn rewarding as a mayor, too—especially a mayor with two kids under the age of three.

Besides its impact on the kids themselves, Birmingham Talks has fostered a community of parents who have become an engaged and vibrant support system for each other, reinforcing the work of the language coaches and being a sounding board for the issues nearly every parent of young children navigates, like screen time. Especially in the aftermath of the pandemic, when opportunities to connect with other parents were still few and far between, our families used the organization as a way to stay in touch, sharing strategies for ensuring that learning continued despite the quarantines. Indeed, one thing I've loved about the program is that, as much as we think of learning as something our kids are tasked with doing, Birmingham Talks is just as much about educating parents.

Since our launch in 2019, we've built Birmingham Talks into an umbrella organization we call Small Magic, which has launched three additional efforts. One of them is called Phonics Power, and it connects parents with literacy experts and resources to ensure their three- and four-year-olds arrive in kindergarten prepared to learn to read.

That's the power of a good idea when it's given a fighting chance: It can take root and blossom beyond what anyone—even its strongest advocates—originally imagined.

The challenge is that, even when city leaders want to do what we did in Birmingham—namely, look to our peers for inspiration in implementing an evidence-based policy—we often lack the resources and support needed to successfully scale it. As part of Bloomberg Philanthropies' tailored replication effort, Birmingham got the help we needed to do both. And now, any city can access similar support as part of an empowering effort called the Bloomberg Cities Idea Exchange.

It's an initiative that accelerates the spread of good ideas by connecting city leaders from around the world who are implementing proven and promising solutions. They can also receive hands-on expert technical assistance to tailor and implement those ideas—from boosting early childhood development to improving air quality to reducing government corruption—something that's vital for public trust and needed for every policy to succeed.

Rather than trying to reinvent the wheel by going it alone or thinking that their coalition is limited by their city's borders, my fellow mayors should recognize that the solutions to many of their most pressing challenges already exist, as does the support to adapt those solutions to their specific communities.

Another example: Results for America's (RFA) Economic Mobility Catalog helps local governments identify solutions that are already proven to work. And RFA's Solutions Sprints have supported nearly two hundred communities in replicating effective solutions.

Programs like these are enabling more leaders to do more good for more constituents—constituents like a grandmother in Birmingham who goes by Ms. Connie.

Ms. Connie has been part of the Birmingham Talks community for years, using the word pedometer to make sure she's showering the grandkids she takes care of not just with affection but with words. At the end of her weekly program sessions, she leaves with a new book—yet another perk of participating in the program. Then she goes to sit in the parking lot with her grandchildren, not because she needs to take a call or her car won't start, but because the kids won't let Ms. Connie drive anywhere until she's read them the latest book.

"A child who has that level of excitement about reading," Ruth Ann

Moss once told me, "the world belongs to them." I agree. And I couldn't be more excited that kids across Birmingham—and hopefully soon, across the country—can benefit from these research-backed interventions.

It's a testament to the power of words, the power of caring adults—and the power of local government to learn, adapt, and deliver what works for residents.

8

A WHOLE GREATER THAN THE SUM OF ITS PARTS

JENNIFER BLATZ,
CEO, STRIVETOGETHER

ALAN COHEN,
FOUNDER AND CEO, CHILD POVERTY ACTION LAB

TODD WILLIAMS,
CHAIRMAN AND CEO, THE COMMIT PARTNERSHIP

Many of the stories in this book are about good ideas—policy initiatives supported by evidence that, when correctly implemented, can make a measurable impact. And this story, too, will involve the kind of government action that often leads to success: in this case, the 2019 passage in Texas of House Bill 3, which made marked increases in education funding tied to data-driven strategies.

But this chapter isn't really about the importance of putting more money into public schools. Nor is it about the reforms that accompanied those extra dollars—reforms that had been proven effective in Dallas before being adopted statewide. It's about the development of an entire ecosystem: a constellation of government, private sector, and organizations including—but by no means limited to—the three we run, which are all devoted to improving outcomes for children. Working together, we have surrounded a problem: a lack of economic mobility among young people in the Dallas area. And we have taken coordinated action to address it. It's been one small step after another in the hopes of achieving a giant leap forward for an entire community of kids.

In many ways, this story begins in Cincinnati in 2006, when a group of local leaders (including Jennifer) came together to design a new program that would help kids in poverty prepare for college—their ticket into the middle class.

It was a county coroner who focused the conversation by standing up and framing the issue differently. "As long as we remain program-rich and systems-poor," the coroner said, "we will not get more kids into college. And what's more, I'm going to keep seeing dead kids on my table."

The group realized that they needed to find a new way of achieving better outcomes for the kids they cared so much about. Instead of launching another new program, they needed to find a way to work together to drive change in all the systems that touch kids' lives. They began working together under the umbrella of an organization they called Strive Partnership, partnering with three school districts in Cincinnati and northern Kentucky to work on improving educational outcomes. Strive Partnership wasn't yet another new program. It was the beginning of a new civic infrastructure devoted to finding and doing what works and expanding it to reach more kids.

Over the next few years, relying on data to drive continuous improvement, Strive Partnership got results. More kids were showing up prepared for kindergarten. Fourth-grade reading and math scores increased. High school graduation rates went up.[1] And other communities across the country noticed. Whenever they reached out to Strive Partnership to ask for advice, Jennifer and her fellow leaders told them the same thing: This only works if you're willing to set aside your own individual ideas and initiatives in favor of a collective approach to impact. The whole has to be greater than the sum of its parts.

In 2011, Jennifer helped to launch StriveTogether, the largest national network of communities devoted to this collective impact approach, and to improving outcomes for kids "from cradle to career." Again, it's important to understand that StriveTogether doesn't prescribe a specific set of actions or policy reforms for each community in this network. Instead, place-based partnerships connect nonprofits, employers, schools, philanthropy, and more, bringing together neighbors to build a stronger future for their community.

In the StriveTogether model, communities monitor seven population-level outcomes: kindergarten readiness, early-grade reading, middle-grade math, high school graduation, postsecondary enrollment, postsecondary completion, and employment.[2] They then use this data to drive collaboration among cross-sector leaders to improve systems ranging from education to housing to health care—all with the goal of securing better outcomes for kids and families. StriveTogether's theory of action is rooted in the idea that true systemic change requires an entire ecosystem of programs and organizations united in vision, committed to continuous improvement, guided by community engagement, and, critically, driven by data and evidence.[3]

Today, with Jennifer at the helm as CEO, StriveTogether is working in more than seventy communities across the country. These communities are united around one goal: elevating four million more young people on a path to economic mobility by 2030.[4]

Four million is a lot: It's enough kids to fill every seat in every Major League Baseball park three times over. And there's no magic bullet to secure that many improved futures. We don't have an "Economic Mobility for 4 Million Kids" bill waiting to be passed at the state or federal level. What we do have are leaders like Todd and Alan in communities like Dallas.

Todd grew up in Dallas, attending public schools and paying for college with the help of Pell Grants before embarking on a twenty-year career with Goldman Sachs. Ever mindful of his origins, he had always been an advocate for public education, sponsoring scholarships for high school students and helping to establish a public charter school in the area.

But when Todd retired from Goldman in 2011, the landscape for public education—and, really, for kids in general—in the Dallas area was bleak. In the 2011 legislative session, the state of Texas cut $5.3 billion from public education, with more than half a billion dollars trimmed from Dallas County alone.[5]

This retrenchment couldn't have come at a worse time for the county's fourteen public school districts. Already, only around a third of third graders were reading at grade level. Just 15 percent of high school graduates were completing postsecondary degrees within six years.[6] Meanwhile, the superintendent of the Dallas Independent School District (ISD) had just left, meaning the district would have its ninth leader in twenty years. And school board elections were being canceled because nobody wanted to run for the seats.

The bigger picture: In one of the nation's fastest-growing regional economies, employers were being forced to import talent from elsewhere, while Dallas's own young men and women were growing up without the tools necessary to compete for those good-paying jobs. Less than a quarter of young adults between the ages of twenty-five and thirty-four were earning a living wage.[7]

Todd decided to devote his full energies to tackling this problem. He agreed to chair a Dallas Independent School District task force focused on finding savings in the district budget. He became a critical education advisor to Dallas's new mayor, Mike Rawlings, as the city struggled to do more with less. And, in September 2011, he and the mayor launched a new organization called the Commit Partnership.

Todd shared Jennifer's commitment to systemic thinking—he's a believer in the management expert W. Edwards Deming's aphorism that every system is perfectly designed to get the results it gets.[8] And he had no intention of letting Commit become yet another organization devoted to admiring the problem of poor student achievement. He wanted to drive systemic change. And early on in Commit's existence, he had a conversation with leaders at StriveTogether that ultimately resulted in an extremely productive partnership.

Todd and the Commit team, which included Alan, quickly defined the organization's mission: figure out exactly why Dallas was failing to put its kids on a pathway to economic mobility, develop and adopt a specific set of data-backed best practices, and serve as a backbone for a network of local institutions all working together to inspire and leverage government action. Looking at the landscape, Todd realized that hard data was the missing piece. In order to achieve the collective impact model he learned from StriveTogether, Commit would need to recruit and hire a dedicated team of analysts focused on leveraging data insights. And to do that, the organization would need to successfully compete with the private sector for the very best talent.

Another lesson from StriveTogether: Collective impact efforts often go belly-up in their early stages because they fail to make much actual impact. As broad as the challenge was, Todd knew that Commit couldn't make the mistake of being a mile wide but an inch deep—in order to gain credibility and build capacity, the partnership would have to quickly start putting some points on the board.

One clear place to dive in was early childhood education. Commit launched an ambitious effort to get more children in Dallas County enrolled in pre-K.

Commit set a clear goal: Ensure that at least 80 percent of Dallas County's children were deemed kindergarten-ready by 2025. They leveraged data: Commit examined the eligible population and enrollment data and provided guidance to its partners on the target population. Government took action: The state legislature approved $130 million for districts whose pre-K programs met certain quality standards. Commit activated a network of partners: Libraries, food pantries, churches, businesses, and other entities blanketed the community with more than one hundred thousand flyers soliciting sign-ups. They engaged the community: A Commit partner called Groundwork DFW held "Feedback Friday" sessions where community members could provide feedback. For example, after hearing that many parents had concerns about the safety of their kids, Groundwork piloted putting cameras in pre-K classrooms to help build trust. And success was achieved: Pre-K enrollment spiked by thousands over the next few years.[9]

All in all, since Commit's founding, Dallas County has seen a 16 percent increase in the number of eligible children who participate in pre-K programs—and students who enroll in such programs are more than two times more likely to meet kindergarten-readiness benchmarks. This is, in part, a success story about the Texas state legislature being persuaded to finally loosen its purse strings and provide some grant money for early childhood education. But it wouldn't have been possible without Commit and its network of partner organizations surrounding the problem, bringing data and evidence to the table, and working together to make a measurable impact.

➔➔

The Texas state legislature only meets for a few months every two years, which means that chances to pass policy initiatives are relatively rare and fleeting. But in 2017, education advocates launched a furious push to reverse some of the 2011 cuts with a piece of legislation called House Bill 21 that would have increased state funding for public schools by $1.5 billion. The bill, however, ran straight into a dynamic that had long kept the legislature paralyzed on school funding. Advocates wanted as much money as possible with as few restrictions as possible—while fiscal conservatives, arguing that more funding would simply be throwing good money at bad results, demanded systemic disruption. When the state Senate cut proposed funding nearly in half and added a voucher provision, the bill stalled.[10]

It was a devastating setback. By then, the National Education Association had ranked Texas thirty-seventh nationally for education funding. And the shortfall was translating into disappointing outcomes among students: Less than one in four eighth graders was achieving a postsecondary credential within six years of their scheduled high school graduation, and postsecondary completion rates for students experiencing poverty (who accounted for six in ten of all public school students) stood at just 12 percent.[11]

Here we had a state with a booming economy that led the nation in job growth—but had to rely on talent who had been educated elsewhere, while Texas's own sons and daughters struggled to keep their heads above water because they just couldn't compete for these good-paying jobs.

At first, Governor Greg Abbott's creation of a thirteen-member bipartisan Texas Commission on Public School Finance might have seemed like a classic example of sentencing something to death by committee. There had been plenty of these "blue ribbon commissions" in the past, few of them useful—but this one was designed to be different.

As a member of the commission, Todd saw an opportunity to bring data and evidence to the table.

The state had set a goal of 60 percent postsecondary completion. And in its testimony to the commission, Commit looked backward through the educational pipeline in search of leaks. One important pivot point, the data found, came in the third grade. Students who weren't reading at grade level by then were three times more likely to drop out before finishing high school than kids who were. But in Texas, only 40 percent of third graders were meeting state literacy standards.[12] If you really want more young adults to get good jobs, Commit insisted, you have to teach more third graders how to read.

By 2018, Commit had established itself as an authority and a resource for policymakers. Since its early childhood work, the organization had grown to include a staff of roughly fifty (now seventy-five), and it had brought in more than two hundred partners from the public, private, and social sectors. In Dallas County, where its efforts were focused, the organization had spearheaded a drive to identify the most effective educators and pay them more to work in struggling schools.

And it had helped to implement the Dallas County Promise, which provides free postsecondary tuition pathways to more than twenty thousand high school seniors each year.[13]

In addition to relying on data and leveraging Commit's work in the Dallas area to illustrate a vision for success, advocates on the commission were careful to make their coalition as broad as possible. The commission brought in the business community by pointing to state projections showing that Texas would have to add as many as 7.8 million jobs by 2036 in order for its employment rate to keep up with the predicted population growth.[14] And it heard from teachers, not just about the challenges of educating for low compensation in crumbling facilities, but about what was working and what would be necessary for those practices to scale.

In all, the commission heard more than eighty hours of testimony from more than 155 stakeholders ranging from state officials to classroom teachers and from charitable foundations to businesses. And at every step Commit was there, working to keep partners organized and supplementing the very human stories with hard data.

In the end, the commission made thirty-five recommendations in a 164-page report that included dozens of data-packed appendices. So when the legislature gathered in January 2019 to draft a bill, not only were both the House and Senate education chairs on board with the core language of the legislation, but much of their work had already been done for them—thirty-one of those thirty-five recommendations made it into the final bill. Meanwhile, Commit and its partners united under a new coalition called InvestEdTX and, with financial support from StriveTogether, turned to pushing for the bill's passage.

House Bill 3, as it was known, could have fallen apart like its predecessor, 2017's House Bill 21. But it didn't. Differences on the details of pay-for-performance for teachers and funding for third-grade reading were hashed out as the bill moved toward passage. Nobody threatened to pull their support just because they didn't get everything they wanted. Everyone understood that alignment was critical—and that the data spoke louder than anyone's individual agenda.

And, in the end, Governor Abbott was able to sign into law $6.5 billion in new public education spending—increasing per-student base funding by roughly 20 percent, funding full-day pre-K for four-year-olds, and incentivizing merit pay programs for teachers. "This one law," said the governor, "does more to advance education in the state of Texas than any law that I have seen in my adult lifetime."[15] Indeed, while 43 percent of Texas third graders were reading at grade level in 2019, when the bill was passed, that number was up to 50 percent in 2025.

➡➡

In addition to increasing baseline funding, House Bill 3 included a trio of data-proven policy measures designed to improve education in Texas:

- The Teacher Incentive Allotment (TIA) was designed to recruit and retain great teachers and incentivize them to work at struggling schools by providing a way to earn six-figure salaries.
- The College, Career, and Military Readiness (CCMR) Outcomes Bonus provided additional funding for school systems that put more of their students on a path to postsecondary success.
- The Additional Days School Year (ADSY) program added funding for elementary schools willing to extend the school year in order to

> ameliorate learning loss stemming from the Covid-19 pandemic and prevent the "summer slide" often seen in students who lose some of the achievement gains they made the previous school year.

The challenge, then, was getting school districts to take advantage of these programs. Having successfully pushed for passage of the bill, Commit and its partners pivoted into implementation mode, launching an organization called the Texas Impact Network to encourage superintendents and principals to buy in.

It wasn't always easy. Many systems had been relying on the same teacher-pay formulas, the same postsecondary guidance programs, and the same school calendars for decades. Todd and his allies had a lot of difficult conversations with school leaders who were unsure about change. And, in the end, it was often data that made the difference. Many superintendents had never seen disaggregated data illustrating what their former graduates were earning compared to the rest of the state, and some were reluctant to take accountability for outcomes they couldn't fully control.

In the end, however, the meetings and conversations paid off. More than three hundred school systems across the state have fully implemented the teacher incentive program, with dozens more on the way, and according to research from Texas Tech, the program "demonstrate[s] positive impacts on both teacher retention and student achievement."[16]

More than two hundred districts have taken advantage of the Texas Impact Network's professional learning communities that are designed to maximize implementation of the college, career, and military readiness program. According to the network's 2024 annual report, students in those districts were more likely to enroll in postsecondary education and attain an industry-based credential.[17]

Meanwhile, nearly one hundred school systems have expanded their school years to take advantage of the new state funding, and according to research from the Texas Education Agency, students who attended an additional twenty-five school days experienced an average gain of 17 percentage points in math proficiency.

➡➡

The story could end there, with the successful passage and implementation of school funding that will get more kids into pre-K, more kids reading by third grade (25 percent more in Dallas since Commit's founding in 2011),[18] and, in time, more kids getting their diplomas.

But this story isn't just about education funding, because the challenge for Dallas County isn't just about education. Out of 3,100 counties in the United States, Dallas ranks seventh for the number of young adults living in poverty and sixth for the number of children living in poverty.[19]

As Todd found himself reminding superintendents and principals almost constantly—and as both StriveTogether and Commit have built into their mission statements—the goal of all this isn't just to get more kids across the graduation stage but to put them on a path to economic mobility. What happens inside the schoolhouse is of the utmost importance to achieving that goal, but there are plenty of other obstacles that must be overcome in order for those efforts to pay off.

That's where our third coauthor—Alan Cohen—comes into the story.

Mayor Rawlings, whose personal investment in education led to the creation of the Commit Partnership, was also laser-focused on the causes of, and potential solutions to, poverty among young residents of Dallas. The two issues, of course, are deeply related, and there's hard data to support that relationship: Poor kids simply don't perform as well in school as their more well-off classmates, which means they lose out on opportunities to lift themselves up into the middle class, which means the generational cycle of poverty continues.

As Mayor Rawlings understood, a great neighborhood absolutely needs a great school. But a high-performing school also needs a strong, healthy community around it. And in 2017, the mayor asked Alan, a former school district official, to launch an organization devoted to the rest of the economic mobility story.

The role of the new organization—called the Child Poverty Action Lab or CPAL—was clear. The mayor committed to convening a sort of children's cabinet, bringing together the heads of every department for regular principal-level meetings. The lingua franca at this table would be data, and CPAL would be the player responsible for generating and propagating that data.

In some ways, CPAL would function like Commit, serving as the linchpin in a collective impact approach to a broad challenge. But unlike Commit, CPAL wouldn't do education work, per se. Instead, it would follow the data to discover where the biggest impact on children could be made. Early on, Alan and the CPAL team identified five "big bets"—five potential levers of economic mobility for children: benefits delivery, maternal health, housing, criminal justice, and safety.

And while Commit would bring to the table a series of proven strategies for improving education, ranging from investment in early childhood education to pay-for-performance for teachers to better advising for postsecondary pathways, CPAL would be free to function as a sort of research and development department for the city—again, going wherever the data suggested in search of new solutions.

If Todd is guided by the Deming quote about systems being perfectly designed to get the results they get, Alan is similarly guided by a quote from Indira Gandhi: "Have a bias toward action—let's see something happen now. You can break that big plan into small steps and take the first step right away."[20]

In order to understand exactly how CPAL does that, look to the corner of Malcolm X Boulevard and Marburg Street in Dallas.

In 2019, CPAL launched a major effort to combat a critical threat to the well-being of children and families: a rising tide of gun violence. Knowing that violence was concentrated in a small set of neighborhoods —and that, even within these neighborhoods, it was concentrated on particular streets—CPAL's analysts took the city's 385 square miles and split the terrain into 110,000 individual microneighborhoods, which they referred to as "cells." Counting up all the cells in which there had been at least one homicide in the last five years and at least three acts of gun violence in the previous year, CPAL identified a total of forty target cells.

These cells represented just 0.03 percent of the city's surface area—less than a sixth of a square mile in total—but accounted for more than 10 percent of the city's homicides over the past five years. The team then added a quarter-mile border around those cells, making them just a little bigger, and the resulting microneighborhoods accounted for nearly a quarter of the city's homicide total.

That kind of data gave the city an enormous amount of leverage, allowing it to solve a problem at scale without having to worry about actually scaling a solution. Solving gun violence in one cell could make a measurable impact on the overall number. Using CPAL's data, that's exactly what the city did at the corner of Malcolm X and Marburg. They installed streetlights, cleaned up abandoned lots, and supported neighborhood mutual-aid projects, cutting the rate of violence by 23 percent. CPAL and its community partners helped, too: Knowing that violence tended to spike in the summer—and that the presence of positivity often creates an absence of negativity—they descended upon one abandoned lot and effectively threw a summerlong community block party.[21]

The net result: Over a two-year period, this cell, which once ranked first in the city for gun violence, dropped to 463rd.[22] And citywide, homicides declined by 13 percent in 2021—even as the murder rate rose sharply in other Texas cities like Austin and San Antonio.[23]

Critically, the efforts of these three organizations—StriveTogether as the national network sharing best practices across jurisdictions, Commit as the leading edge of a collective fight for better educational outcomes, and CPAL as the data specialist helping to identify corresponding pathways to economic mobility—weren't siloed. Indeed, they are often complementary.

As an example: We know from data—and from common sense—that the kinds of educational outcomes prioritized by StriveTogether and tracked by Commit are impacted by a variety of external factors, among them housing stability. It just makes sense that having to move midyear would have a negative impact on educational achievement—parents are distracted by the logistics of relocation, kids are distracted by needing to make new friends, teachers may be at a different point in the textbook in a new school. And the effect isn't limited to young children: CPAL found that students at Dallas College who experienced evictions were more likely to drop out and less likely to reenroll.[24]

Roughly forty thousand households face eviction each year in Dallas County alone.[25] If we could lower that number, we could remove an enormous barrier to educational achievement and the economic mobility that comes with it. And, working with a partner called the Dallas Eviction Action Center (DEAC), CPAL found a way to do just that.

Examining data from the Justice of the Peace courts where eviction filings are adjudicated, CPAL researchers identified a solvable problem. Most renters didn't have legal representation—and without it they had less than a one in three chance of achieving a positive outcome, which was no surprise since most of these proceedings were pro forma and often over within five minutes. However, in the rare cases where tenants were able to find legal representation, their chances of staying in their homes rose to more than 85 percent.[26]

In other words, more legal representation for tenants facing eviction would mean fewer evictions, which, in turn, would mean better educational outcomes at every stage.

Eviction-filing data is public but not easily accessible—or at least, it wasn't until CPAL dug in. Working with Dallas County, the organization began to generate real-time data so its partner DEAC could send postcards offering free legal representation to potential evictees. Often, these postcards would arrive before the actual eviction notices, giving tenants a chance to come to court prepared. DEAC even stationed lawyers at each of the ten Justice of the Peace courts where eviction cases were heard, literally stopping tenants on their way into the courtroom to ask if they wanted free help.

In 2024, DEAC represented more than five thousand families

this way, winning a clear majority of its cases and saving thousands of Dallas-area children from the educational setbacks that come with housing instability.

A few years ago, Commit and CPAL codified their partnership by launching a joint plan called Opportunity 2040, which marries the organizations' twin missions. The plan is to place 150,000 more Dallas County students on a path to economic mobility by the year 2040 while simultaneously reducing the number of children living in poverty by half.

And if the launch of Opportunity 2040 gives Todd and Alan a chance to spend more time working together, you can be sure that Jennifer and the StriveTogether team won't be far away. Indeed, as a national network, StriveTogether can play a critical role in syndicating the success found in places like Dallas to its members across the country. As you've seen throughout this book, good ideas travel, and success can be contagious when an organization like StriveTogether is helping to make it possible.

So there will be more good ideas. More pressure on legislators to live up to their promises on education funding. More opportunities for kids to get ahead. And, ultimately, more young people in Dallas and beyond achieving pathways to economic mobility. One community at a time, that lofty goal of 4 million doesn't seem so daunting.

Fifteen years after StriveTogether developed a national model for supporting government action through collective impact efforts, that model is proving to be stronger and more powerful than ever. In Dallas and around the country, organizations like ours are proving that when we work together—and when government does its part—we can be more than the sum of our parts.

9

ACCOUNTABILITY ACROSS ADMINISTRATIONS

MAYOR MONROE NICHOLS (D-TULSA)

FORMER MAYOR G.T. BYNUM (R-TULSA)

Every community has a defining challenge. This is ours.

The story you're about to read—the story of how two mayors from different backgrounds and different parties have each worked to address a century-old injustice—is decidedly incomplete because its happy ending is yet unwritten and, indeed, unrealized. But it's a story about progress. It's a story about how leaders can earn the confidence of their constituents. And, of course, it's a story about harnessing the power of data and evidence to achieve the ambitious vision we share for the city we both love.

The story begins in the years after Oklahoma first became a state in 1907, when our beloved Tulsa was home to one of the wealthiest Black communities in the entire United States.

It was Jim Crow policies that first forced Black entrepreneurs to congregate in an area known as Greenwood, just north of downtown. But it was inspiration from Booker T. Washington that led them to create a self-sufficient localized economy that supported thousands of middle-class families.

Their "city within a city" was commonly known as Black Wall Street. Inside the redbrick buildings there, you'd find every kind of business imaginable: banks, movie theaters, doctors' offices, restaurants, and all manner of retail stores. The money spent by members of the community, whether on basic services or luxury goods, largely stayed in the community, raising living standards for all. Black Wall Street was a thriving commercial hub and a source of enormous pride for a people living under the boot of segregation.

Then came the night of May 31, 1921.

Some of the details are lost to history, but the basic facts were these: A young Black man, accused of assaulting a young white woman, was arrested, and rumors began to circulate that he was to be lynched. Within a few hours, large groups of Black and white men gathered around the jail—some looking to protect the rights of the accused, others looking to take justice into their own hands. Somewhere in the crowd, a gunshot rang out. Chaos ensued.

However it started, what happened next is stamped permanently on Tulsa's memory. A white mob descended upon Black Wall Street and burned it to the ground. Over the next twenty-four hours, more than thirty-five blocks of the Greenwood neighborhood were laid to waste. More than 1,100 homes and businesses were lost. Thousands of people were left destitute or homeless. And dozens lay dead—local authorities reported thirty-six at the time, but the real death toll may have been as high as three hundred.[1]

You cannot be a citizen of Tulsa, let alone its mayor, without reckoning with the overwhelming physical, economic, and psychic damage our city absorbed as a result of what became known as the Tulsa Race Massacre. That's why, for generations, we have worked to bind the wounds of that horrific moment in our history.

But how can we ever hope to right such an enormous wrong, especially when so many opportunities for justice have slipped through our fingers? Nobody was ever arrested for their role in the massacre, and because no perpetrator remains alive there is no obvious legal avenue to hold the guilty fully accountable. Meanwhile, there has never been any financial recourse for the businesses whose claims were denied by insurance companies, and no compensation has been given to the families whose economic lives literally went up in smoke during the massacre. And while city leaders (of both parties) have long promised a campaign of rebuilding and restoration in the Greenwood district, residents have learned the hard way to greet those promises with skepticism.

Before G.T. could roll out a comprehensive plan to address the massive injustice left over from the massacre, he had to start by earning the confidence of Tulsans. And that started by gathering as much information as he could about the state of the city and its residents—information that directly led to solutions, some of which were surprising.

That's why, early on in G.T.'s administration, the city partnered with the Gallup organization on something called the Gallup-Tulsa CitiVoice Index. This was, essentially, an opinion survey—the most in-depth opinion research that had ever been done in our city. More than 4,400 Tulsans answered the survey, contributing invaluable data about their lives and their feelings about the direction of the city.

One dismaying—if not shocking—finding from the study was that, a century after the Tulsa Race Massacre, citizens of Greenwood were still struggling, relative to their fellow Tulsans. In fact, an earlier study had found that the average life expectancy in the neighborhood was a full eleven years shorter than elsewhere in the city. Despite all the money the city had spent building health infrastructure, people were still experiencing a wide and inequitable range of poor outcomes.[2]

So what was going on? Well, one factor—as revealed by survey responses—was that citizens of Greenwood were less likely to feel comfortable leaving their homes. Your first reaction is probably to assume that it must have been crime that was keeping people indoors. That was what we figured too. But data has a way of leading you down a chain. And when the city asked follow-up questions, the answers came as a mild shock.

For one thing, people said there weren't enough streetlights to make it feel safe out on the streets—a problem that seemed easy enough to fix. But a surprising number of Greenwood residents shared another complaint: Too many loose and stray dogs were roaming the neighborhood. These dogs were walking, barking symbols of urban blight. But they were also literally making residents less healthy by discouraging them from taking walks, frightening children into staying home from school, and causing any number of other associated problems.

We went further down the data rabbit hole, analyzing calls to Animal Control and discovering that people tended to report the most stray dogs between the hours of five and seven at night, as well as on weekends. This made sense—stray dogs don't keep to a schedule, but people do, and that's when people would be most likely to be home and see them. It was easy to imagine someone having come home from a long day at work, contemplating the idea of a restorative and energizing walk through the neighborhood, seeing a pack of mutts outside their window, and deciding to flip on the TV instead.

But then came a key insight: The city had been making a small but important mistake. Our Animal Control officers, like most city employees, worked nine to five, Monday through Friday. Which meant that, when people would call in the evening, officers wouldn't be dispatched until the next morning; when they called on the weekends, there wouldn't be a response until Monday. This, in turn, meant that the problem wasn't really getting solved.

Shifting the work hours of the Animal Control department required buy-in from the city's civil service—and a bump in the budget to account for overtime—but it was an easy pitch when we drew a line directly from the schedule of our officers to the life expectancy of our residents. It didn't fix every problem in Greenwood—indeed, as you'll read, it would take an all-of-government approach to even envision a comprehensive solution—but it was as good of an example as you'll ever find of data-driven policymaking in action.

G.T. will happily confess here that he is a data nerd. He comes by that status honestly. After college, he moved to Washington to work as an aide to a pair of Republican senators: Don Nickles and Tom Coburn.

Senators Nickles and Coburn were often referred to as "archconservatives," but they were really just deficit hawks who honestly and fervently believed that every single dollar of taxpayer money spent by the government should be not just accounted for but also held to account. We should cross-examine every line item on the budget, they taught their young aide, and so G.T. learned not just how to read a budget but how to read into one, and how to envision the people who lived behind the numbers.

Right around that time, President George W. Bush was inaugurated, and he brought in Mitch Daniels as the director of the Office of Management and Budget. Mitch was a businessman and academic who shared that approach to budgeting and understood that you couldn't properly evaluate a budget without good data. So he implemented what became known as the Program Assessment Rating Tool

(PART)—which went on to examine more than one thousand federal programs, scoring them each on a set of objective criteria.

If PART failed to capture the imagination of the American people (or the attention of Congress), it found a fan in young G.T. Bynum. Why *wouldn't* you want to know if the programs you were funding were working? And why *wouldn't* you use all the data you had available to find out? Mitch Daniels became, and remains, a hero of his.

Not long after G.T. moved home to Tulsa, the city councilor in his district retired and he decided to run for his seat, serving on the city council for eight years and quickly developing a reputation as "the budget guy." G.T. liked the moniker, but he avers that he was no Mitch Daniels, just a geeky, bespectacled, young politician pushing for more performance audits and nudging city government toward a more data-driven approach.

At some point, he was invited to participate in a Results for America fellowship program where he met fellow data nerds from local governments across the country. As the fellows eagerly compared notes on their work, he realized something important. G.T. had always thought of data as an effective tool for budgeting. But in the right hands, it could be so much more—a vehicle for helping people get past the partisan divisions that inevitably occur in government by bringing things out of the realm of philosophical debates and down into the realm of practical problem-solving. It could be a cure for politics as usual.

So that's what he ran on when he ran for mayor in 2016—a year in which, to put it mildly, a boring, nonpartisan approach to government was not exactly in fashion. G.T. was running as a Republican against the Republican mayor in a pretty Republican city, and the incumbent went more or less nuclear, sending out mail pieces linking G.T. with Hillary

Clinton. The young challenger decided to stick with his message, promising to deliver not just results but data illustrating those results—and won by seventeen points. On election night, G.T.'s phone kept lighting up with texts from his fellow Results for America alums, who were thrilled that a bona fide data geek—one with the self-described "raw animal magnetism of a young Orville Redenbacher"[3]—had managed to get himself elected as mayor.

Getting stray dogs off the streets was just the beginning of G.T.'s data-driven work to improve outcomes in the Greenwood neighborhood.

As he said in a TEDxPennsylvaniaAvenue talk in February of 2017, "We are bringing every tool that we can to address this life-expectancy disparity, and we're not checking party registration cards at the door to the meetings. We don't care who you voted for for president if you want to help restore the decade of life that's being stolen from these kids right now."[4]

And he knew that relying on data and evidence would be key to fulfilling that promise.

But he quickly discovered that the city had a grand total of two city staffers dedicated to data-backed policymaking, and they were mostly doing management trainings for their fellow employees, not really weighing in on big policy decisions. The new mayor decided to pivot that little operation into a real data team and, critically, he was able to recruit a local transportation planner named James Wagner to run it.

In many ways, James is the hero of this story; he's a creative, forward-thinking leader who is always totally committed to getting results for the people he works for. He was the one who came up with the idea of putting out an open call on social media, inviting anyone with any expertise or interest in collecting or analyzing data to volunteer for what became known as the Urban Data Pioneers (UDP).

James thought we might get a handful of people to show up, but dozens came to the very first meeting, and in time we had more than one hundred people join the UDP. It was a real eye-opener. All around us, it turned out, we had a tremendous reservoir of people, many working in city government, others working in banks and hospitals and energy firms. These were data geeks just like us, people with a unique set of skills that nobody had ever asked them to deploy for the good of the community—until now.

So out they went, counting potholes and timing traffic lights, and very shortly they began to make a big difference. One early example: The UDP quickly found that higher levels of education were the predominant driver of higher income in a particular city tract. Now, our state has a program that pays for four years of college—a great deal, but one that's only available for eligible high school seniors who fill out a byzantine set of paperwork. Very few of our high school seniors were going to the trouble of filling out these applications, so we saw an opportunity. Working with the local chamber of commerce, we launched a drive to get more kids signed up—increasing the percentage of high schoolers applying by more than 10 percent.[5]

Another example: One of our priorities was finding a way to make Tulsa a more stable place to live by cutting down on the number of evictions suffered by our people. The volunteers at UDP dug into more than fifteen years of water utility billing records and analyzed when people had their water cut off—an early indicator of financial problems that eventually led to eviction. They also built a predictive regression model, which showed that the biggest indicator suggesting an eviction was imminent was if someone was unable to pay their late fees. With just a little bit of data geekery, we had identified a lever we could pull to help keep folks in their homes.

But the biggest issue in our city, as identified by the Gallup survey, was the condition of our road infrastructure. It had been at the top of the city's agenda since G.T. had been a city councilor. But it wasn't until we started using data that we began to correctly prioritize these repairs. The Urban Data Pioneers noted that it didn't make sense to treat two roads as equal priorities if one had one hundred times as many people using it on any given day. But they went beyond merely pointing out the problem by building a tool where the council and the mayor could plug in different variables and create a list of which streets should be fixed in what order, taking into account not just the condition of the pavement but any number of other factors.

Within a couple of years, the road repair program was working so well that, when the mayor put forward a bond for the largest street repair investment in city history, it passed by a historic margin.

This didn't feel like politics as usual—or even government as usual. It felt like real problem-solving. And over time, we built that approach into every part of city government.

In addition to the development of our citizen data brigade, another important early step was the creation of regular meetings where department heads would gather to present and share information. We'd seen other cities do this—Louisville had LouieStat and Baltimore had CitiStat—and G.T. wanted Tulsa to have the same opportunity, so we created TulStat. At first these meetings were kind of a slog—one

PowerPoint after another. Department leaders needed time to realize that TulStat wasn't an excuse to bring in a bunch of number-crunching consultants intent on eliminating jobs but rather an opportunity to break down siloes and shorten lines of communication—we adapted the format to fit our city's needs. And the mayor made sure the team knew that attending every single TulStat meeting in person was a nonnegotiable item on his calendar.

➡➡

All of this helped to establish city government's credibility with everyday Tulsans. But none of it addressed the challenge that was always lurking in the background. G.T. knew he would be in office during the one hundredth anniversary of the Tulsa Race Massacre, and he wanted to do something that went beyond merely acknowledging the tragic date.

When he came into office, the city worked with the Rockefeller Foundation to create the Resilient Tulsa Strategy, our first-ever strategic plan to combat inequality in our city. We also created a new office for resilience and equality so there would be people coming in to work on the problem every day—and we hired a woman named Krystal Reyes, who would go on to be Monroe's deputy mayor, to run it.

As always, data was key to our work. We partnered with City University of New York (CUNY) to create what we called the Tulsa Equality Indicators, which measure equality across a broad range of variables like race, gender, veteran status, housing status, and more. That's how we initially discovered the eleven-year life expectancy gap among residents in the Greenwood neighborhood.

We focused the bulk of our economic recruitment incentives around that part of the city. And when we talked to companies about coming to Tulsa, we emphasized that we didn't just want to see them put up a cool-looking building that people could drive past on their way to low-paying jobs elsewhere in the city. We wanted them to be part of addressing the community's broader challenges. Some companies shied away from that demand. Others embraced it, including the two largest new employers in Tulsa's history.

In G.T.'s first few years as mayor—with a comprehensive strategy ranging from job training to economic redevelopment to, yes, getting those stray dogs off the street—we cut that life expectancy gap from eleven years to four. (Then came Covid, which exacerbated these inequality issues, especially in health care. But even then, we were able to use data to encourage people to mask up and get vaccinated.)

This all laid the foundation for the launch of the Kirkpatrick Heights & Greenwood Master Plan. Around that one-hundred-year anniversary, we began thinking about how to redevelop fifty-six acres of publicly owned land north of downtown that had been taken by government authorities decades earlier for the purpose of "urban renewal" but never really used to any great effect. We spent sixteen months developing the plan, including forty meetings and events engaging more than one thousand Tulsans—because all the data in the world can't be substituted for getting buy-in from real people.

By the time we rolled out the plan, G.T. was facing down the end of his second term and beginning to think about life after public office. So the city created an organization called PartnerTulsa to guide the redevelopment going forward, and G.T. hoped that the next mayor, whoever he or she turned out to be, would keep us on the right path.

That new mayor turned out to be Monroe. But while we come from different political parties, both of us love numbers. Monroe's staff will tell you that he thirsts for relevant information when he's trying to solve a problem.

The new mayor believes that values-driven data delivers the best outcomes for residents, regardless of their zip code. His background is in place-based partnerships—for example, he worked for StriveTogether, an organization featured in chapter 8 of this book. For Monroe, statistics are not just a means to an end—they work to quantify problems and, importantly, show the efficacy of the solutions so that the community as a whole can address them.

By the time Monroe was running for office in 2024, people were looking for a more expansive vision of government than they'd been in the market for back in 2016. After eight years of political tumult on the national stage—not to mention a pandemic and the resulting economic crisis—Tulsans wanted their local government to do more. They picked a Democrat to lead the city next, one who would build on the data-driven nature of G.T.'s administration and who laid out real policy goals that were driven by data and a call for accountability for outcomes.

As the newly elected mayor, Monroe was determined to uphold the culture of accountability developed under his predecessor, but he also had an ambitious agenda to fulfill. So when he took office, he laid out six key goals for his administration—not broad policy visions, but specific performance indicators he wanted city government to hit:

- Achieve functional zero homelessness by 2030.
- Bring six thousand new affordable housing units online by 2028.

- Make Tulsa the safest big city in the country.
- Improve student outcomes to put fifteen thousand more of Tulsa's children on a path to economic mobility.
- Expand economic opportunity in every part of the city.
- Markedly improve our work to cogovern with Tribal Nations.

These wouldn't just be the mayor's goals. They would be the goals of every employee of the city. The new administration brought new energy and a new way of looking at how policies implemented for years could fit the goals that Tulsans so enthusiastically voted for.

A good example of the culture came when the city's chief data officer left. Monroe decided to pivot that office into a Department of Performance and Accountability because he wanted it to be more than an aggregator of information. He wanted someone there who would hold his feet to the fire and let him know if we were doing a good job on any given issue at any given moment. But he was keenly aware that you can't have a Department of Performance and Accountability if you've never had a chief data officer. Without G.T.'s commitment to collecting information, Monroe wouldn't have been able to instill the culture of accountability he wanted in city government.

Under the new administration, we continued the trend toward gathering more information by launching the Neighborhood Conditions Index (NCI), a block-by-block survey of key data. It's like a regular blood test you get at your doctor's office to check your cholesterol. Through the NCI, we're able to stay on top of residents' top issues, which, by the way, continue to include animal services (now its own department). But we marry the data with qualitative information we can only get by going out into these neighborhoods and talking to people about the realities of their lives.

On June 1, 2025—six months after the transition between our two mayoral administrations and 104 years after the Tulsa Race Massacre—Monroe stood before a crowd of Tulsans and announced a new plan to help Greenwood, and all of Tulsa, move forward on a "road to repair." The city, he announced, would create a private charitable trust with the goal of securing $105 million in assets to spend on housing assistance, building improvements, land development, small business grants, and scholarships.

The media noted that he went out of his way *not* to refer to the plan as "reparations"—a deliberate choice that was made in order to avoid some of the difficult political connotations that come with that word. But John Hope Franklin, the American historian and native Tulsan, once said, "If the house is to be set in order, one cannot begin with the present; he must begin with the past."[6] In the audience that day were the two living survivors of the massacre: Ms. Viola Ford Fletcher and Ms. Lessie Benningfield Randle. They had seen their neighborhood burned to the ground. Tulsa was determined to ensure that they would see it rise again.

Monroe knew that some thought he was asking a lot of Tulsans when he announced that plan, but many, regardless of race and geographic location, were eager and enthusiastic about Tulsa being the catalyst to move beyond apologizing and into direct work to improve the lives of community members. Most of all, he knew that the community had to trust the process, which is why he decided on a charitable trust instead of using public funds. Taking it out of the conversation around public funding cooled temperatures and political dynamics.

We do that every day as public servants—ask for people's trust. We ask for it explicitly when we run for office, of course, but we need it to do anything of consequence once *in* office. And the trust the new mayor was asking for had been slowly built over the course of the eight years preceding his arrival in office.

That's why we decided to write this chapter together. One of us is a Black, progressive Democrat; the other is a white, conservative Republican. We don't share a lot of ideological preconceptions. But we do share a belief that trust can only be present where there is accountability. We both understand the role data and evidence can play in instilling a culture of accountability in city government. And, ultimately, while we may have different visions of what government should aim to accomplish, we both share a commitment to results-driven policymaking that has allowed Tulsa to prosper under both of our administrations.

Politics may often seem like a tug-of-war. A Democrat is elected and immediately begins to undo what his Republican predecessor did, or vice versa. In our case, however, we both see city government as a relay race. And as one of us takes the baton from the other, we see great things in our city's future. As Monroe said in his inaugural speech, "Some of our challenges may be new; what it will take to meet them might also be unfamiliar and at times uncomfortable, but the values of hard work, honesty, tolerance, curiosity, perseverance, and hope that it will take to dispose of them are baked into our DNA as Tulsans."[7]

Tulsa is a great community with a proud and complicated past—but one with a brighter future than generations before might have thought possible.

10

FOLLOW THE EVIDENCE: CONNECTING AMERICANS TO GOOD-PAYING JOBS

PLINIO AYALA, CEO, PER SCHOLAS

ASSEMBLYMEMBER AMANDA SEPTIMO (D-NEW YORK)

The federal government runs more than forty workforce development programs spread across fourteen agencies, with annual spending reaching approximately $17 billion. Democrats and Republicans alike will tell you over and over again: Workforce development is a critical piece of the puzzle when it comes to generating economic mobility.

But for a long time, the government's approach to workforce development has boiled down to three words: *train and pray*. Instead of focusing on *outcomes*—how many people actually find good-paying, fulfilling jobs as a result of their participation in a workforce development program—we have a tendency to settle for *outputs*, simply running as many people through a curriculum as possible and hoping for the best.

What if we told you we could do better? In fact, what if we told you about a program that *is* doing better?

That program is called Per Scholas, and the evidence for its success is clear, objective, and undeniable.

Consider the following:

- More than 80 percent of Per Scholas graduates find full-time employment in the technology sector within a year of completing the program[1]—and, last year, they recorded the largest number of job placements in the program's thirty-year history.[2]
- Randomized controlled trials demonstrate the effectiveness of Per Scholas's programs. Participants earned nearly 20 percent more than control groups over seven years and were half as likely to rely on government assistance such as TANF, SNAP, housing, or unemployment benefits.[3]

- By increasing lifetime earnings by an estimated average of $1.8 million for each graduate, Per Scholas achieves an eight-to-one economic return for every dollar invested in the program.[4]

Per Scholas is a proven success story that's playing out in more than two dozen communities across America, helping tens of thousands of people—especially people of color in low-income neighborhoods—gain a foothold in fast-growing fields like cybersecurity, IT support, and cloud computing.

This enormous success is evidence of what's possible when workforce development programs are aligned with the needs of employers and targeted to support workers in communities where opportunities are scarce. But this is also a story about government—and what happens when government *follows* the evidence.

When government leaders in city halls and state houses across the country *demand better results*—and invest in programs that deliver—we unlock the greatest source of economic mobility: the human potential that exists in all of our communities.

In order to do that, government needs to help programs like Per Scholas grow. It needs to respond to evidence of success by shifting funds in the right direction, away from programs that aren't working. And it needs to sustain those investments over time as programs evolve to become more successful at delivering results.

The two of us are proud to boast that Per Scholas grew up where we did: in the South Bronx, a neighborhood long defined in equal measure by the richness of its culture and the poverty of opportunities that limit its residents.

Growing up amid empty lots and abandoned buildings on 178th Street, off Tremont Avenue, Plinio learned an important lesson that has stayed with him for life: Talent is everywhere—opportunity isn't. The kids he grew up around were every bit as smart, every bit as motivated, and ten times tougher than the kids down on the Upper East Side. But chances to climb the economic ladder were few and far between.

Then, as now, there was only one way to escape that kind of poverty: a good-paying job. And education was the only path to find one. Plinio was lucky enough to have an English teacher who took a special interest in him, helping him earn a scholarship to a school in Manhattan and a path to college. When he graduated, he built and sold a small business before returning to the South Bronx, looking for a way to pay it forward.

In 1998, he found his opportunity in Per Scholas. The organization had begun a few years earlier when John Hoyt Stookey and Lewis Miller, two strangers on an airplane, got to talking about their mutual interest in technology—and in lifting up underserved communities like ours. They began collecting unwanted used computers and fixing them up to donate to families and schools in the Bronx. Per Scholas even operated a retail storefront in Plinio's old neighborhood, where they sold and repaired technical equipment.

Back then, it was all about improving digital access for people who didn't have it. But as technology became an increasingly important sector of the American economy, Stookey and Miller saw opportunities to help people directly participate in the boom by providing them with the IT training they'd need to find good-paying jobs and pursue meaningful careers in technology.

All these years later, a lot has changed—both in Per Scholas's operational model and in the world of technology. But the organization's core value proposition remains the same. Per Scholas offers a full-time training program that runs for two to four months, with a mix of hands-on and instructor-led learning, virtual courses, and broader professional development. Its learners, the vast majority of whom are people of color from disadvantaged neighborhoods, never pay a dime—but they leave with a wealth of resources. They achieve industry-recognized certifications, they are given specific assistance to land jobs with employers who have helped design the curriculum for the openings they need to fill, and they leave with a renewed sense of purpose and valuable life and career skills ranging from financial literacy to resume building to conflict management.

➡➡

To a government leader like Amanda, that kind of value proposition is extremely attractive, especially because she represents the South Bronx, where residents—despite their deep pride in their tight-knit community—face high levels of food insecurity, asthma rates that are eight times greater than the national average, and the highest unemployment rates of any of New York's five boroughs.

But she also has a personal reason to believe, and invest, in the Per Scholas promise: Her brother is a graduate.

Like Plinio, Amanda grew up knowing that education was the key to escaping the cycle of generational poverty—indeed, her parents insisted that their children would go to college. But while Amanda thrived after high school, her brother struggled. It wasn't until he signed up for a Per Scholas program that he found his path forward. She will never forget him beaming as he walked across the stage in his best suit at their graduation ceremony. Even better: Practically stapled to that diploma was a job offer from a hedge fund that wanted him to work in their IT department. He's since received a promotion and three raises—and he's saving up to buy a house at the age of twenty-nine.

Stories like these are common among Per Scholas graduates. Take Joovay Arias, who enrolled in college as a computer science major, but couldn't afford the tuition and soon dropped out to seek full-time work. An arrest on his record made that difficult. But Joovay persevered, working seventy hours a week fixing cars until he could no longer handle the physical labor.

At a crossroads, he began driving for Uber and Lyft. It was a passenger who first told him about Per Scholas, and Joovay was accepted into its eighteen-week Codebridge Software Engineering course in New York. He'd train all day, stick around on campus to finish his homework, and drive during evenings and weekends to pay his bills. He was able to graduate with a new level of discipline, a strong creative portfolio under his belt, and offers from Google and Spotify. He turned a tech fellowship at the latter into a full-time programming job.

"I have always loved computer science," Joovay said, "but thought it was just for college kids in California. Now I realize that if you study hard, you can make it!"[5]

For Amanda, this kind of story is one of the most valuable tools in the toolbox when it comes time to advocate for government funding for organizations like Per Scholas.

Like so many of her fellow new-generation lawmakers under the age of forty, she sees enormous opportunity for her constituents in the digital revolution. In a modern world where everything that we do is technologically focused, everything from health care to education is delivered in some digital format or another. The kind of training available at Per Scholas, then, is giving people the skills not just to survive but to thrive in communities like the South Bronx, driving the upward economic mobility we want for all our families.

That's why she's made the case for Per Scholas on the floor of the state Assembly, in private conversations with her colleagues, and while promoting Per Scholas at workforce fairs in her district office. Some people respond well to the data, some to the human stories—and Per Scholas has both in spades.

Because of all the evidence supporting its model, over the last two years, Amanda and other supporters in Albany have helped secure more than $2.4 million in funding for Per Scholas from the state government. New York City has chipped in over a million dollars as well. And Per Scholas is now poised to serve more than 1,200 learners at its Bronx campus, in 2026 alone.

Amanda is also working to help Per Scholas expand throughout the state. In 2024, thanks in part to a grant from Empire State Development, a state workforce development agency, Per Scholas was able to open a new campus in the historic Larkinville district of Buffalo.

Out of the eighty-four participants enrolled in Buffalo's Per Scholas classes in 2024 and 2025, approximately sixty have already landed full-time jobs—which equates to $3.5 million in annual income.[6]

One of them is Lennon Williams, a Buffalo resident who had attempted to self-teach coding but struggled to gain proficiency without support. One day, while scrolling through social media, he came across a video for Per Scholas. He scrolled right past it—only to find that someone else had seen the video and shared it with him. It felt like a sign.

Lennon was part of the inaugural cohort in October 2024, and he says he "fell in love with it—the material, the instructors, and the mission." During the program, he earned his CompTIA A+ certification and, thanks to a mock interview hosted by Per Scholas's career-development team, he was able to secure a good-paying IT job after graduation as a functional support analyst with Odoo. Now he and a fellow Per Scholas graduate are building out a tech network in Buffalo that is aimed at connecting tech professionals, employers, and aspiring learners. "I didn't even know what I was capable of," he says, "until I joined Per Scholas."[7]

As for the organization, it's now expanding its Larkinville campus, adding on more classrooms as well as opening a satellite office in Rochester.

At key moments in Per Scholas's history, government support has made a crucial difference. An investment from the Obama administration's Social Innovation Fund—earned in the wake of a Public/Private Ventures impact study confirming that Per Scholas alumni significantly outearned their peers[8]—served not only as a source of funds but as a key validation, showing foundations and corporate sponsors the value of the program. Since then, Plinio and the Per Scholas leadership team have been able to expand the organization to twenty-five campuses in nineteen states across the country. And everywhere the organization goes, it adds to its track record of achieving measurable results—and inspiring stories.

For example: Back in 2011, the primary economic development entity in Columbus, Ohio—called Columbus 2020—predicted that, within the decade, the region's economy would add 150,000 new jobs, with many of them being good-paying tech jobs. This was great news, but it came with a catch: Most of those jobs would only be available to people with an associate degree or an equivalent credential.

This put those jobs out of reach for too many of Columbus's neediest. Over the past twelve years, the poverty rate in the city had increased by 50 percent. More than one in five people were living below the federal poverty line, with households of color making up a disproportionate share of those in poverty.[9]

It was a frustrating dilemma. On the one hand, you had employers with good-paying jobs to fill. On the other hand, you had a city full of people thirsting for good-paying work. Supply and demand seemed not to match.

In early 2012, Per Scholas leaders came to town and established relationships with a pair of city council members. They served as validators and facilitators, introducing the organization to members of the Franklin County business community. Per Scholas was able to raise initial funding from the city, as well as from area employers and trade associations, and, in October 2012, it welcomed its first cohort of twenty learners in Columbus.

Two months later, those learners were graduates. They would go on to pursue—and secure—full-time jobs at companies including JPMorgan Chase, Nationwide Insurance, and Time Warner Cable.

In 2022, as the region struggled to bounce back from the economic disruption caused by the pandemic, Franklin County—having identified women of color as a group especially in need of help—invested $4.5 million in American Rescue Plan funds to support a Per Scholas initiative called Tech Women of Color.

One of these women—we'll call her Sally—came to Per Scholas after working at a shoe store for eleven dollars an hour, a wage she simply couldn't live on. She attended programming for fifteen weeks in the spring of 2022 and graduated into a job at a company in Columbus that paid her seventeen dollars an hour. A month into her time there, Per Scholas formed a partnership with Nationwide, which wanted to hire apprentices for a software development program. The organization reached out to Sally and invited her to take another course, which she was able to complete remotely during evenings and weekends, and she wound up getting one of those apprenticeships—which paid twenty-two dollars an hour. Six months later, she was hired on full-time. Now she makes six figures doing amazing work at Nationwide and comes back to talk to Per Scholas graduates regularly. Her message: *Yes, it's possible.*

These initial investments—coming from city council members, state legislators, and the federal government—have helped Per Scholas establish a significant foothold. But, for Amanda, one of the most important reasons to keep funding Per Scholas is that the organization continues to evolve as it grows, following the evidence as it seeks to meet the current and future demands of employers, especially in the age of artificial intelligence, which is now a core component of the Per Scholas curriculum.

For example: As the organization was beginning to grow, Plinio recognized that it was excluding potential learners who lacked the financial stability to participate in a full-time program. So Per Scholas worked with Social Finance, a grantee of the Google Career Certificates Fund, to launch what it calls the Zero Percent Loan program.

It's a $3,000 loan with no interest and no strings attached. The learner can use it however they need. And then they pay it back over the course of three years once they've landed a job and are hitting a certain earning milestone. If something happens and they lose their job during that period, the loan goes into forbearance. And at the end of three years, no matter how much they've paid back, the remainder is forgiven.

This has allowed a larger pool of people to participate in the program—Lennon Williams being one of them—and early evidence is proving that people who are taking advantage of the "zero percent loan" are graduating at higher rates and getting jobs faster. It sometimes takes more than education to get to that first paycheck, and Per Scholas is helping to smooth the way.

Another evolution of the model has to do with the work that comes after someone has gotten that elusive first job. During the pandemic, Per Scholas leaders realized that simply getting someone a job wasn't the endgame. They wanted to help people build and move along career pathways—encouraging them to think about their second job, and their third, where the real money is. So the organization instituted a new initiative called Career Accelerator, where it's offering very intentional upskilling opportunities to graduates in targeted areas that allow them to grow their careers. Last year, Per Scholas trained around 5,500 people—but it also upskilled more than 2,600.

Plinio also evolved the way he makes his pitch to potential business partners. When Per Scholas began, its approach to employers was more from an altruistic lens: *Hire someone from the community—it's a good thing to do.*

But that approach was neither sustainable nor expandable. Plinio realized as he started attaching data to the organization's performance and doing additional research that there was a clear value proposition to employers. Per Scholas was saving them money through the training that it was doing. Graduates were lasting longer on the job than someone else that they could hire off the street. All of that allowed the organization to change and pivot its message to employers. When Plinio approaches an employer now he says, "How can we help solve your hiring problem? How can we build a program together that is effective for you and effective for the mission of this organization?"

Data makes the difference in Plinio's pitch to prospective employers. And, Amanda has found, it can be a difference-maker for legislators as well. Evidence of impact leads to investment—it has in New York and in dozens of cities across the country, including Baltimore, Los Angeles, and Seattle. Because of the organization's ability to evolve to meet the changing needs of its communities, because of the transformational impact it can have on individual learners and entire communities, and, most of all, because of the wealth of data and stories supporting the Per Scholas model, leaders like Amanda are well equipped to argue for more funding.

But we are still fighting an uphill battle to make that case. Right now, approximately 12 percent of Per Scholas's funding comes from the government. The organization aims to more than double that by 2030—so it can triple its impact. In order to do that, we need to convince policymakers both that Per Scholas's methods work and that following the evidence in making government funding decisions really matters.

It matters to Joovay. It matters to Lennon. It matters to Sally. And it matters to people like the ones Amanda represents in communities like the South Bronx. What's more, it matters to their children and to their communities. These are multigenerational payoffs to government investments we can make today—investments in a world where opportunity goes wherever talent can be found.

11

HOLDING OURSELVES ACCOUNTABLE

TENNESSEE COMMISSIONER OF EDUCATION LIZZETTE REYNOLDS

Within the next five years, nearly two-thirds of the jobs in my state of Tennessee will require some form of postsecondary education or training.[1] And across the Volunteer State's 148 public school districts, we spend a lot of time thinking about how to make sure our students are ready for that imminent future.

Simply put: If we want our community to be ready for the jobs of tomorrow, we need excellent schools today—and we have to be willing to do what it takes to get the foundations of education right. We have to make sure every student is reading by third grade. We have to train the next generation of effective teachers. We have to lean forward and help students who are still catching up from the learning losses they suffered during the Covid pandemic. We have to prepare high schoolers for the jobs growing rapidly in our state, from health care to advanced manufacturing.

But it's not enough to say we need to *invest* in these priorities. We need to ensure those investments are actually making the impact they promised. In Tennessee, a state with a long, bipartisan tradition of research-driven innovation in education, we're making a big bet on the future of our nearly one million students. Indeed, since Governor Bill Lee took office, we've invested more than $2.5 billion in public education. And we're determined to make sure that bet pays off.

That's why this chapter isn't just about the money we've invested in our promise to prepare every child in Tennessee for a prosperous future. It's about the steps we've taken to drive accountability at every level, using data to ensure that the reforms we implement are really delivering.

After all, investments without accountability are simply good intentions. Indeed, unless we're actively and continually measuring ourselves against objective targets for improvement—and dedicating our funds to programs that actually *work*—all the money in the world won't make enough of a difference for children. The Tennessee promise is alive and well—and, as you'll see in this chapter, we've got the data to prove that we're actually keeping that promise in schools across the state.

Anyone who knows me knows that my passion for education is deeply personal.

I grew up in Harlingen, Texas, in the Rio Grande Valley, in a family that often struggled to make ends meet. There were times when we relied on government assistance, and paying for basic necessities like the phone or electricity was a constant concern. But even in those difficult circumstances, my parents taught me the importance of studying hard because they believed education was our path forward—and for me, it often felt like the only path to a different life. I was the first person in my family to go to college, and earning my degree opened doors I never thought would be possible. It ultimately led me to a career in education policy as I was driven by a deep conviction that students from backgrounds like mine matter and deserve to be counted, supported, and given every opportunity to succeed in school.

I wound up working for then-Governor George W. Bush, who, when he became president of the United States in 2001, brought together Democrats and Republicans around a vision of ensuring every child had a chance to succeed, no matter where they grew up. Key to that vision was a massive investment in our public schools, which was tied to accountability measures in the form of standardized tests to measure student achievement.

In 2023, I was asked to interview for the position of education commissioner under Governor Lee. I'd never lived in the Volunteer State and had never run a department of education, and I wasn't even sure I wanted the job—until the interview. I came away truly inspired by Governor Lee's personal commitment to both student achievement and the accountability necessary to produce it. Suddenly, I knew where I belonged.

Back in Governor Lee's second year in office—with the education department under the leadership of my predecessor, Penny Schwinn—Tennessee faced a crisis in the form of the Covid-19 pandemic. Schools shut down as states scrambled to stop the spread of the virus, leaving students forced to engage in remote learning. Despite the best intentions of those who wanted to keep schools closed, remote learning simply wasn't working for students in Tennessee (or elsewhere, as evidenced by national scores on math and reading tests plummeting during this era of "Zoom school").

In January of 2021, the governor called for a special session to address the related learning-loss crisis. He knew that, down the line, this gap would result in greater poverty, decreased economic productivity, and even higher incarceration rates. The safety of Tennessee's neighborhoods, the prosperity of the state—and, most importantly, the future of its children—were all on the line.

Speaking to the General Assembly, Governor Lee made the case for action the best way he knew how: with data.

"It would be much simpler to hope or to assume that disruptions to school caused by Covid will just come out in the wash," the governor told lawmakers. "But, unfortunately, the data—the science—tells us that isn't true. Data suggests there are very real consequences to keeping students out of the classroom for this long. Nationally, that looks like a 50 percent drop in reading proficiency and a 65 percent drop in math proficiency with third-grade students."[2]

He also pointed to a survey of more than twenty thousand children across nine states in which fewer than two in five fifth-through-twelfth graders reported that they "learned a lot almost every day" during the shutdown. Nearly two-thirds reported experiencing distractions at home that interfered with schoolwork. Black and Latino students reported facing disproportionately more obstacles to learning at home than their white and Asian classmates.[3]

Tennessee, he concluded, needed to reopen the schools—and it was one of the first states in the nation to do so.

But—critically—it wasn't enough to stop the bleeding. Even before the pandemic, fewer than one in three Tennessee third graders—and just over one in four eighth graders—were proficient in English language arts. Data from the Nation's Report Card showed that reading proficiency of fourth graders in Tennessee had remained flat for the last seven years. When you fall behind at that age, it can be almost impossible to catch up.

That's why, over the course of a five-day special session, Governor Lee and the legislature came up with a plan to pair federal pandemic relief funds with a $160 million grant-matching program in order to fund the creation of TN ALL Corps—a tutoring program based on a proven approach in which students would gather in small groups for short sessions two or three times a week. The content in these tutoring sessions would align with that in core classroom instruction, ensuring everyone was reading from the same page (sometimes literally).

Tutoring wouldn't be limited to the school year, either. Tennessee set up targeted summer camps to help students who were at risk of falling behind, with more than 120,000 students enrolled in summer programs.

Standardized testing in the fall of 2021 indicated immediate improvement over the spring and summer. And within two years, statewide scores showed an amazing, measurable impact: For students in third through eighth grades, English language arts scores increased by eight points, and math scores increased by ten.[4]

The special session also tackled the literacy crisis that had been going on even before Covid-19. You read earlier in this book about the "Mississippi Miracle"—the Magnolia State's commitment to phonics-based reading education that transformed the state's education system. Tennessee had its own version of that same "miracle" after the legislature acted in the special session to tie state dollars to that proven approach to reading education. Nearly every teacher in the Volunteer State now uses the phonics-based method, and the payoff is clear: According to national standardized testing, since 2019 Tennessee is sixth in the nation in fourth grade reading growth and number one in gains among eighth graders.[5]

Tennessee didn't just mandate the use of evidence-backed teaching methods. The state also put $100 million behind Reading 360, a comprehensive literacy improvement initiative, which included a two-summer blitz that trained virtually every elementary teacher using hands-on lessons from their own classrooms. A whopping 97 percent of teachers said it immediately sharpened their instruction.[6] And each year, we're able to see more and more of our kids meeting proficiency as a result.

That wasn't all. During the special session, the legislature also launched the first federally registered Teacher Occupation Apprenticeship, now scaling through sixty-five local "Grow Your Own" pipelines that let aspiring teachers earn a degree, mentorship, and a paycheck (tuition-free), all while working in their home districts. Tennessee's General Assembly passed legislation to support dual-enrollment programs that empower local workforce and education partners to improve the skills of the next generation of Tennessee workers. It also funded local community mental-health centers to provide school-based behavioral health liaisons.

So, when I came to Nashville, I inherited a system that was flush with resources—and full of talented professionals with great ideas about how to spend them. My challenge was making sure we implemented reforms that would drive not just more spending, but better results. Tennessee had designed its education revolution around evidence-based programs. Now it was time to implement them, with the data leading the way.

One of the strengths of our system—and something I rely on every day—is our research partnership with the Tennessee Education

Research Alliance (TERA) at Vanderbilt University. TERA doesn't just partner with our department, but also works with local school districts to turn complicated research questions into actionable findings.

We're also one of the few state education agencies with its own dedicated research staff, including a director of research. This started years ago, and we've maintained our commitment to research across administrations, which is rare in this business. We're deeply committed not just to understanding the evidence base—so we're not swayed by the latest fad in academic circles—but to making a real contribution to the science. And we use this data all the time to make sure we're continually improving.

One landmark step forward came in 2022, when Governor Lee signed into law the Tennessee Investment in Student Achievement Act (TISA). Our old funding formula funded schools based on overall enrollment, staff-to-student ratios, and other related line items. The new formula, created after significant stakeholder engagement, takes into account the specific needs of each student, allocating funds based on the supports needed to best educate each student, including those with disabilities, those who are learning English, and those who come from low-income families.

Another critical step was even longer in the making. Back in 2016, Tennessee was charged with establishing a letter-grade system for schools to provide families with a clear snapshot of school performance and year-over-year progress. Each school would be graded on an A–F scale that emphasized not just overall achievement, but improvement among students ranking in the bottom 25 percent—because we wanted to make sure no one got left behind.

Implementation was delayed for years due to administrative issues and, later, the pandemic, but when I came to the department in 2023,

I made it a top priority to get this school letter-grade system over the finish line. We held town halls all over the state to hear directly from stakeholders—I put thousands of miles on my truck—and, everywhere we went, we made it clear that, in 2023, it was going to get done.

A word here about the nature of accountability: Many people hear that word as a threat. But this was never about throwing stones at school systems. Tennessee's superintendents, principals, and teachers do amazing work—and I'm honored to stand alongside them. We all want to see not just *good* schools, but *continually improving* schools. We can't get there without collecting, analyzing, and, critically, acting on the insights we get from hard data.

So we crunched the numbers—on student achievement, on academic growth, on the performance of the highest-need students, on college and career readiness—and, in December 2023, we were able to release the very first edition of our school letter grades, which we made not just available but easily accessible via a public dashboard.

Doing so wasn't just about putting underperforming schools on notice. It was about empowering parents to better understand how their schools were doing with their children. Many places use accountability to identify areas of success or failure, but we wanted to actually make that connection for our parents.

You can already see meaningful improvements in districts across the state. Alcoa City Schools and the Hollow Rock-Bruceton Special School District have seen double-digit improvements in success rates among elementary schoolers. Alamo City Schools and Clinton

City Schools have seen double-digit improvements among middle schoolers. The Tennessee Public Charter School Commission and Collierville Schools have led the way with double-digit improvements among high schoolers.[7]

In Knox County, under the leadership of Dr. Jon Rysewyk, of the eighty-two schools that received letter grades in 2024–25, more than half earned an A or B, and fewer schools received low marks than in previous years. State assessment data released in June 2025 showed that 44.1 percent of district students scored "proficient" on English language arts assessments across all tested grades, up 4.8 percent compared to 2021–22—news that came as a relief and a delight to area parents and teachers alike.[8] At Christenberry Elementary School in Knoxville—where the motto is "We Rise Up to Become the People We Want to Be!"—I witnessed the immense pride that teachers, administrators, and students felt after being designated a "Reward School," the state's top honor, for its high levels of student achievement and academic growth.

And in Jackson County—a Reading 360 Model District—Director of Schools Kristy Brown, who has since become our state's chief academic officer, supported teachers in implementing the TN Foundational Literacy Skills curriculum with lesson preparation, instructional coaching, and ongoing professional learning, and developed model instructional videos that continue to be available on the department's website today. Brown's early implementation of student supports like TN ALL Corps tutoring and summer camps, in addition to the ongoing work of the district's current director, Jason Hardy, have led to a 13.9 percent increase in overall English language arts proficiency since 2021.[9] Jackson County Schools was recognized as a 2024 "exemplary" district—one of only ten districts to achieve that distinction.[10]

After all those years, the implementation of our letter grades was a significant step forward for accountability and improvement in the Volunteer State. And I'm particularly excited to share that accountability requirements have contributed to the record-breaking reduction in the number of students scoring in the "below proficiency" category for third and fourth grades over the last two years. We're not just raising the ceiling; we're raising the floor—and we're keeping the promise not to leave anyone out of the education revolution in the Volunteer State.

But I don't see accountability as a "one-and-done" kind of thing. Standardized tests like our Tennessee Comprehensive Assessment Program, like our report cards, represent a vehicle for learning and getting better—for helping individual students and school districts to keep improving.

And I don't see accountability as solely the province of state agencies like ours. Federal education policy works best when it reinforces evidence-based practices, supports innovation and research, and helps states like Tennessee share what works through grant funding, technical assistance, and long-term investments. State-led, locally implemented, federally supported, and always research-grounded—that's the way to drive better outcomes.

Data isn't always the world's most exciting topic. And nobody has an abiding passion for forcing kids to take more standardized tests. But this is the work of lifting up children.

And maybe what we're doing in Tennessee can serve as proof for leaders in other states that leaning into accountability can deliver results. Consider that, from 2021 to 2025, the following occurred:

- Overall student proficiency in reading went up from 29.6 percent to 40.9 percent—meaning we've surpassed pre-pandemic levels of proficiency and continued to improve beyond where we were.
- For students in that critical band between grades three and five, reading proficiency went up from 31.5 percent to 43.3 percent.
- Unlike other states that have seen a decline from their initial gains among elementary school students, our eighth-grade scores are showing that we're maintaining those gains into middle school and beyond.[11]

These meaningful and sustained gains resulted not only from continued investment in and implementation of high-quality materials, ongoing professional learning networks, and student supports like summer camps and tutoring, but also from our insistence on measuring for accountability and achieving district buy-in at the state level—all of which worked together to drive these outcomes.

Indeed, we believe that accountability is the foundation of improvement. And under Governor Lee's leadership, Tennessee has been—and will continue to be—a national leader not just in improving our public schools, but in improving outcomes for every student, especially those who grew up as I did.

12

BETTER RESULTS, FASTER: ROCKET FUEL FOR GOVERNMENT

MAYOR MATT MAHAN (D-SAN JOSÉ)

Welcome to the future.

We live in an era of enormous progress made possible in large part by great leaps forward in technological innovation. In the year 2026, cars drive themselves, new cures and treatments are discovered regularly, and you can have nearly anything delivered to your doorstep in a matter of hours with one click of a button. Given the pace of change, it's almost impossible to imagine what else might become possible next year, let alone over the course of our lifetimes.

But this progress isn't happening everywhere—at least not on an equal basis. Look at the private sector, where productivity has surged over the last fifty years and where the pace of change is only increasing with time. Then look at the public sector, where productivity has remained relatively flat. At a time when so much of American life is becoming more efficient, government inefficiency becomes all the more glaringly obvious. Americans see their government as staid, anachronistic—the domain of number-two pencils and mimeographed forms in an age of smartphones. And they're not wrong to feel that way.

Now comes the rise of artificial intelligence, and one of two things will happen. Either AI will continue to exacerbate this gap—with the private sector hopping on the express train to greater productivity while the public sector dawdles in the depot—or it will empower us to close the gap once and for all.

This chapter is about how we in San José, and leaders in communities across the country, are choosing the latter path—and building a brighter future.

I'm excited to tell you about how we're using AI to fill potholes and solve crimes, to make the buses run faster and permitting more efficient, to keep our residents connected to what's going on in city government and empower every single city employee to get more done for the people they serve. But first, I want to tell you why it all matters so much to me.

I ran for mayor in 2022 on a very specific premise about our city's government: I believed we were failing to deliver results because we were trying to be everything to everyone. It's understandable, because when you're in elected office your instinct, not to mention your incentive, is to say yes to everyone and everything: Every stakeholder, every project, every new idea seems full of promise. But I felt like San José was spreading itself too thin, paying lip service to a million different initiatives without driving measurable progress on any of them.

So I threw my hat in the ring. But unlike many insurgent outsiders, I didn't run on a raft of brilliant but untested new ideas. Instead, I ran on a core promise to get back to basics. I wanted us to do fewer things, but do them right. And, on top of that, I wanted to make sure we were tracking and reporting our progress. Coming out of the tech sector, I was obsessed with the methodology of performance management, and I understood the importance of building a team focused on outcomes. Whether you're reporting to a board of directors or a citizenry, it's critical that you are able to regularly show measurable progress on what everyone agrees are the right key performance indicators.

Upon taking office, I took stock and realized that the city was working on more than forty different priority areas on something of a scattershot basis. There was no focus. And it wasn't that any of these priorities were wrong, per se—but if you have forty priorities, you really don't have any. In my first budget message, and in every city council meeting I attended, I insisted that, in my administration, we were going to focus on five key areas: no more, no less.[1]

By now, everyone in city government can tell you what those focus areas are: We want to end unsheltered homelessness. We want to make San José the safest big city in the country. We want to address blight and beautify our neighborhoods. We want to build more housing. And we want to grow the local economy.

Each of these focus areas comes with metrics to track our progress. And if you want to pitch me on something, you have to explain how your idea would move us in the right direction on one of those metrics. If something doesn't fit into any of those areas—well, it might have to take a back seat for the time being.

The reason I'm telling you all this is so you understand that, for me, artificial intelligence can't just be a cool toy. Yes, we're the hub of Silicon Valley, and yes, we have more patents per capita than anywhere else in America, but city government can't just be into innovation for innovation's sake. This has to be about driving better outcomes in key focus areas. AI may be fascinating, but for us, it's a means to a rather timeless end: delivering better services for our residents.

Let me run through a few examples of how we're doing exactly that.

One of our five focus areas is building more housing. California is in the midst of a serious housing crisis that boils down to a simple problem: There just aren't enough places for people to live. One way to solve that problem is to speed up the process by which we assess and approve applications for accessory dwelling units, or ADUs, which are secondary living spaces on the same lots as primary residences. These applications can be complicated, and the homeowners filling them out aren't generally lawyers or contractors. They're just regular people trying to put a mother-in-law apartment on the market. So they make mistakes. We looked into it and discovered that something like 90 percent of ADU applications wind up getting sent back at least once to correct one or more errors.[2]

There's no reason for two human beings to go back and forth in a game of email ping-pong for weeks or even months when we have the technology to put a city planner in your pocket. We built a custom AI tool that flags errors in real time, helping you to submit a correct application on your first attempt and guiding you toward a more successful project.[3] The end result: fewer email threads, quicker approvals, more people served with the same amount of tax dollars—and, ultimately, more available housing units.

Another example involves our local bus system. Without good public transit, it's difficult for many people to get to and from work on time—which means the speed of our buses has a direct impact on our local economy. That's why we partnered with a company called LYT on a pilot project that uses AI to prioritize traffic signals so city buses can avoid red lights and pass through intersections more quickly. In four months, we revolutionized travel on two key downtown bus routes, covering 122 traffic signals over more than twenty miles of roadway and resulting in a 50 percent reduction in red-light delays. Overall, since we started, we've been able to reduce bus travel time in the city by 20 percent.[4] Our buses move faster through town, meaning we can serve more people, better, with fewer vehicles. The city saves money, and our residents save precious time.

We also used AI to create a real-time crime intelligence center, making use of existing cameras to help law enforcement solve crimes. We collect an enormous amount of raw data and empower our analysts to generate meaningful, time-sensitive, and actionable information. I'm proud to say that it's been years since a homicide went unsolved in San José[5]—and that, as of June 2025, more than 80 percent of our residents say they feel safe in their neighborhood, which is an increase of 10 percent since September 2023.[6] In addition, we've put cameras on city vehicles and, while blurring personally identifiable information like faces, these cameras can detect potholes with 97 percent accuracy and trash or debris with 88 percent accuracy.[7] Score one for beautifying our neighborhoods.

One more example: San José is one of the most diverse cities in America. Nearly 40 percent of our residents are foreign-born, and more than half speak a language other than English at home.[8] In fact, we have the largest population of Vietnamese people in any single city outside of Vietnam.[9] So we used to spend hundreds of thousands of dollars a year hiring outside contractors to translate our city meetings into Spanish, Vietnamese, and other languages. We don't do that anymore, thanks to AI programs that allow us to produce high-quality, real-time translations faster, cheaper, and now in dozens of languages. Again, this isn't just about saving money—it's about welcoming all of our residents into the process of city government, often resulting in neighborhood concerns being taken care of faster and more effectively.

Recently, we launched a new initiative called the AI Incentive Program. In August of 2025, we awarded $175,000 in grants to four early-stage companies willing to set up operations in our city.[10]

We received 170 applications, and, to be honest, even I was surprised by how great the submissions were. In the end, we picked four winners based on their civic impact, their growth potential, and their willingness to adhere to ethical standards and responsible deployment practices:

- **Elythea,** a Voice AI platform focused on reducing health disparities and enhancing maternal health and health care for people of color.
- **Metafoodx,** a scalable solution for food waste targeting smaller restaurants and food service companies.
- **CLIKA,** which helps to reduce power consumption by compressing common AI models with little impact on efficiency, thus reducing the demand on our power grid and infrastructure.
- **Satlyt,** a decentralized network allowing underutilized satellites to devote their computing power to supporting AI technology.

One of these companies might wind up being the next NVIDIA—and it will be headquartered right here in San José. But even if these bets don't pay off, the brilliant employees at these four start-ups will enter our talent pool, and they may even start another company or help existing companies in our local economy succeed.

These are all examples of what we call "top-down" implementation, where we identify narrow deployments of AI technology in order to achieve a specific outcome related to one of our key focus areas. And it's exciting stuff. But I think you can really see the promise of AI in the reverse type of implementation, which we call "bottom-up." That's where we expose employees to various tools and frameworks in order to empower innovation at every level of government.

Even in San José, where innovation is in our blood, some city employees got nervous when we started introducing them to AI technology. People naturally worry that the net result of AI is going to be replacing humans with machines. But we don't see AI as a replacement for our city's workforce. Rather, we see it as a force multiplier.

That's why anyone who works behind a desk in our city government has the opportunity to take a twelve-week training course offered by San José State University and the freedom to develop their own custom AI tools to help them do their jobs more effectively.

Our workforce *loves* to learn and grow. At first, we thought about how to incentivize people to take the course—maybe we could give away Sharks tickets or Starbucks gift cards. Turns out, we didn't need to. People were excited to learn how they could develop their skills and make their jobs more effective and satisfying. Already, thanks to this upskilling, we've saved tens of thousands of hours of staff time, and some of our departments have seen productivity rise by as much as 20 percent.[11]

If you want an example of generative AI working hand in hand with our human workforce, come and talk to an employee named Andrea in our Department of Transportation. A few years ago, she used a custom

AI assistant to secure $12 million in federal funding for electric vehicle chargers.[12] But in early 2025, the grant was suspended due to changes under the new presidential administration. That could have been the end of the story. But Andrea was able to quickly pivot, using her new technical skills—and a custom GPT program she created—to apply for and secure a $2.5 million Metropolitan Transportation Commission grant[13] for sixty new EV chargers across six community centers and several libraries in underserved neighborhoods.[14]

When you're done talking to Andrea, pop over to our IT department and ask for Stephen. He'll tell you about our 311 service that residents use to report nonemergency issues—over three hundred thousand of them every year.[15] In order to get requests to the right desks as quickly as possible, the online interface features a drop-down menu of categories for residents to choose from. But we find that people often don't see their issue listed, so they select "other." Someone then has to go through all the "other" tickets and assign them manually to the right desk. Or, at least, that's how it used to work—until Stephen created a custom AI assistant to analyze and categorize these entries. The tool automatically identifies recurring themes like "junk removal" or "water issues" and helps these frequent requests get to the right places. Streamlining this process saves staff more than five hundred hours a year.[16]

We want to see hundreds—thousands!—of San José's city employees taking this course and following in Andrea and Stephen's footsteps by developing their own AI copilots. This investment in our own (human) workforce is at the heart of our AI strategy—we imagine a future in which coming to work for the city is a launching pad to a great career in or out of city government because it's a place where you can upscale your own abilities. AI doesn't have to destroy jobs—it can make them more satisfying and empowering.

Of course, the potential impact on human jobs isn't the only concern around the responsible use of AI. And it's not the only safeguard we've built into our use of the technology to ensure people are protected.

We were one of the first cities in the country to produce generative AI guidelines for our employees,[17] which are contained in a thirty-three-page document that sets the ground rules for using AI. Those rules are simple and clear: We let people know when AI is being used, we don't put personal or private information into our AI systems, we watch out for bias and test our tools, and we take responsibility for what AI creates at our direction. We do not let AI make actionable decisions, like approving job applications or responding to emergencies. And we rigorously examine any new tool to make sure it follows our policies on privacy, security, and fairness.

Back in 2023, as we began implementing our framework for the use of AI, we got used to asking our vendors tough questions about privacy and data use. And we found that other cities were also finding their way through the same issues. We were not alone in wanting to drive responsible implementation of this technology—and we were not alone in wishing there were some kind of guidance we could follow to do so.

That's why we convened more than fifty government agencies from around the country to start sharing best practices and lessons learned—because why start from scratch when so many of us are working on the same issues? What started as a Zoom call with dozens of agencies has grown into a nationwide network called the GovAI Coalition, with more than nine hundred state, local, and federal agencies representing more than 150 million Americans. The GovAI Coalition is a laboratory of democracy—a marketplace of ideas where governments at every level can work together on an open-source basis to exchange tips, share tools, and make public services faster and more effective.

After all, one advantage of this being the public sector is that, unlike in the private sector, we're not in competition with each other. We all want to solve the same kinds of problems. We all want to achieve the same kinds of goals. And so we actually have an advantage over private business when it comes to driving AI because we have hundreds of city and state agencies piloting different programs and sharing intelligence on what works and what doesn't.

And whether it's better implementation—for example, nine cities have contributed twenty-seven thousand language translation pairs to develop a functioning GPT for different languages[18]—or negotiating better terms with vendors to secure the privacy and safety of our data, the GovAI Coalition is already taking what works and spreading it across the country. We happen to be a big city in the heart of Silicon Valley, and we're happy to take the lead on a lot of these issues, but the beauty of our coalition work is that nobody, no matter how new they are to innovation, has to start from zero.

For all the hype around AI, it's worth remembering that machine learning itself is not a brand-new concept. And, taking a step back, technology has always had the potential to drive innovation in the public sector. It's just that, far too often, government leaders have let that opportunity slip through their fingers. Think about how long it took for basic services to move online in the age of the internet.

What's different this time is that leaders like those in our GovAI Coalition are seizing the chance to harness this latest wave of progress. We're establishing commonsense guardrails around our use of the technology in order to earn people's trust and demystify what may seem like science fiction to many—but we're also refusing to let inertia, that frequent bugaboo of the public sector, stop us from innovating.

Ever since we've been governing ourselves, we've been looking for more effective and efficient ways of getting that important job done. Now we have a critical opportunity to deliver better results, faster—a chance to pump some rocket fuel into the machinery of government. I hope our example will inspire others to step up and take advantage.

13

DOING WHAT WORKS IN WASHINGTON

CONGRESSMAN GREG LANDSMAN (D-OHIO)

CONGRESSMAN RUDY YAKYM (R-INDIANA)

So far in this book, you've read one story after another about government using data and evidence to support smarter policymaking and drive better outcomes for everyday people. And we hope that, like us, you've gained a measure of optimism from reading these stories. These examples prove that a better way is possible.

Of course, that optimism may be tempered by more than a bit of frustration. After all, none of the stories you've read so far originated in Washington, DC.

It's true that, for too long, Washington has done too little to ensure that the billions of taxpayer dollars the federal government invests in key programs and policies are delivering their intended results for the American people. We've seen firsthand how often federal dollars flow out on autopilot, without sufficient evaluation or clear evidence of impact.

Ask most Americans about the policymaking process in Washington and the same word keeps coming up: broken. Folks are fed up when campaign promises don't turn into improved outcomes, when rank partisanship prevents us from investing in proven solutions, or when bureaucratic inertia blocks us from delivering better results for our constituents. When Washington fails to invest in what works—or even track the impact of the dollars we've already spent—we lose trust with the people we serve.

We're not here to defend the status quo. As lawmakers from both parties—elected in a red district and a blue district—we were each sent here to shake up the way Washington operates.

We're also not here to concede defeat. In fact, we believe that not only is a better, smarter way of conducting the business of the American people within our grasp, the stars are aligning for a revolution in federal policymaking. As reflected by our partnership, there is broad consensus across the political spectrum that federal programs should be more accountable and results-driven. Democrats, Republicans, and independents agree on what needs to be done. And we are proud to be leading the fight for real, substantive, meaningful change—not in some far-off future, but today.

So we hope you'll indulge us in one more story—a story full of promise and potential, but one whose ending is yet unwritten.

This isn't a new idea. As you read in the introduction to this book, the federal government has taken at least a casual interest in using data and evidence to make smarter decisions dating back decades. And in 2016, that interest resulted in a meaningful step forward, as conservative Republicans and progressive Democrats teamed up on a piece of legislation called the Evidence-Based Policymaking Commission Act.

As its name suggests, the bill established a federal Commission on Evidence-Based Policymaking that was assigned to examine the government's capacity to collect, analyze, and report out information about the effectiveness of federal programs.[1] The commission, to be made up of fifteen experts from across the political spectrum, would evaluate the idea of creating a federal "clearinghouse" for program and survey data, allowing researchers and policymakers to use that data creatively to reach conclusions and inform decision-making. Commission members were also tasked with resolving a key challenge to the promulgation of federal data—namely, how to make the data more widely available while still preserving the privacy rights of people who interact with federal agencies.

The bill sailed through Congress, receiving unanimous approval from the Senate, and was signed into law by President Barack Obama. And soon the commission began its work, holding its first public meeting in July 2016. Over the course of the next eight months, the panel would hold three public hearings and six more public meetings, hear from forty-nine invited witnesses, and convene presentations to solicit input from more than forty organizations.

The commission's final report, issued in December 2017, was a landmark document in the fight for results-driven policymaking. It laid out a comprehensive strategy for addressing the biggest challenges standing in the way of smarter decision-making in Washington: a lack of access to the data itself, insufficient privacy practices to protect people if and when that data became more widely available, and inadequate capacity to generate the very evidence policymakers were supposed to be using to guide their actions.[2]

In one section of the report, commission members laid out a litany of questions whose answers should be guiding federal policymaking, except that the data to find those answers was unavailable. What effect was nutrition assistance having on health outcomes? Did job training provided by the military result in improved earnings for veterans? Was the Farm Service Agency doing a good job helping farmers get credit? We didn't know because we weren't collecting and analyzing the data correctly.

The report made a series of recommendations to address this

challenge. Notably, it suggested that instead of simply establishing a repository for federal data, Congress should establish a National Secure Data Service—akin to the Congressional Research Service—so that researchers and policymakers could work hand in hand to find answers and evaluate programs. The report also suggested a set of protocols that could be put in place to protect data privacy—thus overcoming a key hurdle—and recommended that each federal agency designate chief data officers, evaluation officers, and statistical officials tasked with making sure the right data was available, accessible, and ready to be analyzed at any moment.

There was little fanfare surrounding the release of the report—no ticker-tape parades down Fifth Avenue, no breaking news coverage on TV. Most people, even in Washington, probably didn't even notice it among the swirl of news at the end of the year.

But leaders in both parties and in both houses of Congress had been waiting for this moment for a long time. And when Congress came back into session at the start of 2018, they acted again, teaming up on a piece of legislation called the Foundations for Evidence-Based Policymaking Act, usually referred to simply as the "Evidence Act."

This new bill was designed to codify into law many of the recommendations the commission made in its report. It required federal agencies to appoint officers responsible for coordinating the collection and use of federal data, promoted an open and accessible data system with strong privacy protections, and developed the federal government's understanding of how to ask rigorous evaluation questions.

Notably, while the first bill we mentioned was signed into law under President Obama, the Evidence Act bore the signature of President Donald Trump. It was a major statement about the bipartisan nature of the drive for smarter policymaking and a major step forward in measuring and improving the impact of federal programming. At two dozen federal agencies, things began to change. Officers were appointed. Protocols were put into place. Data began to flow.

The Evidence Act built a foundation for evidence-based decision-making across the federal government. But none of this guarantees real change—only the *opportunity* for change. While Congress appropriates buckets of money, federal agencies have also traditionally exerted influence over how dollars are allocated. And, at a more basic level, it's true that you can't use data that you don't have—and collection of that data is an executive-branch function. Still, while ramping up the role of data and evidence within federal agencies is an important step forward, the real prize would be carving out a similar role in the *legislative* process.

That's where we come into the story.

Together with our colleagues Congressman Blake Moore of Utah and Congresswoman Brittany Pettersen of Colorado, we launched a "What Works Caucus" in 2023. With equal membership from both parties, we built the caucus around a shared goal: ensuring that taxpayer dollars are invested as efficiently and effectively as possible to improve outcomes for children, families, and communities nationwide.

We share some things in common. We're all relatively new to Washington, first elected in either the 2020 or 2022 elections. We're all in our forties, which makes us practically children by DC's standards. But we all came to this fight from different perspectives.

One of us (Rudy) comes from a business background, where spending wisely instead of wastefully can be a matter of survival for a company. Indeed, upon arriving in Washington, I observed that the federal government is the only entity that simply renews spending each year without going back to evaluate whether the previous year's spending on a given project was actually effective. I signed up to help lead the caucus as part of my commitment to cutting the skyrocketing national debt and helping Congress fulfill its responsibility to allocate the tax dollars of hardworking Americans to what works, not what wastes.

The other of us (Greg) is a former teacher and city council member. As such, I was motivated by the high expectations of my constituents, who, as I heard in my visits back home to the district, have too much on their plates to worry about whether government is actually working. Given the wealth of information available to Congress and federal agencies, I felt that the American people were right to expect that their government would use data and analytics to deliver better results. Like the rest of us, I also saw the promise of the caucus to help turn down the partisan temperature by finding common ground around investing in programs that have the greatest impact.

Together we launched the caucus because we believe, as have so many who came before us, that if federal policies and legislation are grounded in—and prioritize—evidence of what works, we can make better decisions and faster progress on our toughest challenges.

Under our joint leadership, the caucus has convened policy experts to advance ideas for improving the return on taxpayer dollars and the effectiveness of government programs. We welcome members from across the political spectrum to develop and promote results-driven, evidence-based legislation and innovative partnerships. We spotlight data-driven efforts at every level of government, as well as the work of partners in the private and social sectors. Wherever results are being delivered, we go.

One early priority was to build support for a resolution establishing a congressional version of the Commission on Evidence-Based Policymaking, except this one would be charged with exploring how data and evidence could better be used in the legislative process.

Members of our caucus have also worked together on legislation like the Evidence-Based Grantmaking Act,[3] a bipartisan bill to help Congress and federal agencies invest in what works. The premise is simple: Each year, federal agencies award more than $150 billion in grants intended to improve economic outcomes for the American people—yet less than one-quarter of this grant funding is directed toward programs supported by evidence.[4]

This bipartisan legislation would set new requirements to ensure that taxpayer dollars are consistently invested in projects with a strong track record of success, that federal programs have clearly identified outcomes and goals, and that these programs are frequently and impartially evaluated to make sure they are delivering results for the American people. Programs must commit to these basic requirements if they want to be awarded discretionary grants, which is the mechanism that's responsible for distributing that giant pot of money each year.

We also resolved to support individual pieces of legislation that reflected a data-driven approach—and the success of the bipartisan approach to implanting results-driven leadership at federal agencies. For example, Indiana used the US Department of Transportation's SMART grants program, which rewards states and cities for using data to reduce traffic fatalities, to tackle the problem of work-zone intrusion and enhance safety for drivers and workers. Meanwhile, the 2021 expansion of the federal Child Tax Credit resulted in dramatic reductions in child poverty across the country. These models can be replicated and scaled with the right federal guidance.

And while we built support for legislative vehicles, we also have been hosting trainings for congressional staff on how to use evidence creatively, highlight progress happening at the state and local levels, and exchange ideas for how to bring more data to the table in everything we do.

It's early days—Washington still moves at a snail's pace when it comes to meaningful reform—but we're already excited about the progress we are starting to make together. Neither of us was here when the Evidence Act passed. But we're ready—eager, in fact—to keep embedding data and evidence into the programs, policies, and processes that Americans rely on.

Here's what we've learned so far about the importance of building evidence, investing in what works, and shifting funds away from what doesn't.

First, evidence improves efficiency and effectiveness. Actual oversight and accountability doesn't mean cutting programs just for the sake of it—it means intelligently funding programs that deliver results. When we prioritize outcomes, we can identify programs that are failing to deliver on their promises and take steps to either fix them or replace them with programs that are rooted in data and evidence. That's not ideology; it's common sense.

Second, it encourages innovation while learning from failure. No program will succeed 100 percent of the time, but by evaluating what works and what doesn't, agencies can adapt, improve, and scale success, and phase out what doesn't work. That kind of honest and flexible culture of learning and experimenting is what the public sector needs more of, not less.

Third, it restores public trust. Americans want to know that their tax dollars are making a difference and, perhaps more importantly, not going to waste. When federal programs are transparent about their goals and rigorous about measuring progress, it sends a clear message: This government is serious about delivering for you and your family.

In 2024, our work became even more important when the Supreme Court's ruling in *Loper Bright Enterprises v. Raimondo* overturned the so-called Chevron Doctrine. The decision limited federal agencies' ability to interpret ambiguous laws through regulation, handing more power—and more responsibility—to Congress to be specific about how it wants federal money spent.[5] There's never been a better or more important time to embed data and evidence into the legislative process.

Indeed, at the end of the day, all of this work reflects a simple, universal truth: Good policy is built on good information.

Whether you're a Democrat, a Republican, or an independent, a mayor or a lawmaker in Washington, the decisions that impact your constituents should be based on the best available information—not politics, not inertia, and certainly not guesswork.

The American people are realists—they don't expect perfection from their government. But they do expect it to learn, improve, and deliver. By setting evidence and data as the North Star for how we design and fund public programs, we can move closer to a smarter government that lives up to its promise—one that solves problems, earns trust, and gets better with time.

CONCLUSION

WHAT IT TAKES TO DO WHAT WORKS

MICHELE JOLIN, CO-FOUNDER AND CEO, RESULTS FOR AMERICA

DAVID MEDINA, CO-FOUNDER AND COO, RESULTS FOR AMERICA

As a nation, we spend over $1.5 trillion annually on vital, government-funded programs intended to open doors of opportunity, including investments in education, workforce, housing, health, and more. Yet the American Dream is fading for too many. As the Opportunity Insights data on economic mobility shows, where you live—and what zip code you are born in—play a powerful role in shaping your future life outcomes, and too many people and their communities are left out of America's economic success.

The issue is not a lack of resources—and it's not that our challenges today are too large or too intractable to solve. The issue is that too often we do "what we've always done," despite the enormous evidence about what *actually* works to drive upward economic mobility that has been developed over the last decades by researchers, governments, nonprofits, and others.

Most government decision-makers, no matter their ideological orientation, want to get better results. The challenge is not a lack of intention. Instead, as this book illustrates, too often government decision-makers are frustrated by the complex information landscape that makes it hard to find what works, the structural barriers that make it difficult to fund what works, and the political barriers or bureaucratic inertia that make it difficult to change the status quo and do what works.

As the chapters in this book have demonstrated, there are steps that all government leaders—at all levels of government—can take to overcome barriers to delivering results and open opportunities for all.

First, **define success and follow the data and evidence to do what**

works. Governments need to identify outcomes that will actually improve residents' lives, and then use evidence-based, data-driven solutions to drive toward those outcomes. Sounds obvious. But too often that is not what happens. At the federal, state, and local levels, government agencies operate enormous portfolios of programs, often with overlapping purposes. Each agency—and many times each program—independently defines its intended outcomes. Meanwhile, evidence is not consistently used to guide decisions toward better results and agency data systems do not connect to offer a shared view of progress toward key outcomes. The result: Governments are attempting to solve complex problems using disconnected or outdated information and multiple funding streams that are not aligned to deliver results.

As chapter 8 in this book describes, the Commit Partnership and the Child Poverty Action Lab partnered with state and local government leaders to set community-wide targets for reducing childhood poverty and increasing jobs with a living wage—challenges that the community in Dallas identified as key to improving economic mobility. In Mississippi, then–Lieutenant Governor Tate Reeves and former Superintendent of Education Carey Wright understood that academic success for all children depended on being able to read by third grade, and they followed the Science of Reading to spark big gains for children in Mississippi. Other states have learned from this, and a number of them, like Commissioner Lizzette Reynolds's Tennessee, are seeing positive results. When Mayor Mike Johnston set out to tackle Denver's homelessness crisis, he established clear citywide goals to measure success and was able to lean on a body of research showing that a Housing First policy would be effective, helping him to overcome political obstacles to achieving his targets.

Many of the problems facing America's communities have been solved by government leaders elsewhere, so governments need to learn from others rather than reinvent the wheel. As Mayor Randall Woodfin spotlighted in his chapter, he is not ashamed to tell you that Birmingham Talks, the highly successful early-literacy program in his city, is based on an evidence-based idea that was first implemented in Providence, Rhode Island. He sought out implementation lessons from peer governments and adapted the city's program to meet the unique needs of his community. Governments increasingly value this kind of idea sharing and cooperation. Just look at the GovAI Coalition, described in San José Mayor Matt Mahan's chapter, which is making it easier for government leaders to exchange tips, share tools, and build on each other's ideas.

Second, and very importantly, **create incentives in public funding to do what works.** Governments have powerful funding levers—through budgeting, grantmaking, procurement, and contracting processes—to shift taxpayer dollars to solutions that work. Yet funding decisions too often reflect historical allocations, statutory formulas, or program activity rather than measurable impact. Instead, as this book illustrates, government leaders need to create incentives to achieve outcomes and prioritize evidence and data in funding decisions, helping them break from what has been done before and do what works. In Chicago, as this book describes, it was changing the terms in a city grant through a request for proposals (RFP) that helped city leaders deliver more effective youth mentoring to thousands of young people. In Ohio, Governor Mike DeWine insisted that state agencies use evidence and logic models in the budgeting process to ensure taxpayer dollars were directed at investments with a history of, or strong rationale for, delivering better outcomes. Tennessee leaders used budgeting and grantmaking levers to expand evidence-based programs like high-impact tutoring, which have helped reduce pandemic-related learning loss. And from the South Bronx to dozens of communities across the country, results-driven government leaders have steered public funding to Per Scholas, a program with evidence and a track record of success, putting tens of thousands of young people on a path to well-paying careers in growing employment sectors.

When government dollars are wasted on ineffective programs, it is often the most vulnerable communities that bear the brunt of unmet needs and missed opportunities. Failing to direct public funds toward solutions that work widens growing economic inequities and is a profound societal and moral failure that further breeds mistrust in government.

Finally, **build a culture that supports all government decision-makers to do what works.** Many of the success stories in this book are not just about a government program or two—they are about a leader setting a government-wide tone emphasizing that results matter and creating a culture that allows all government decision-makers to do things differently. When Governor Wes Moore took office in Maryland, he did not just institute a few new initiatives to improve Maryland government—he set out to redirect the entire state government to deliver better results. In Tulsa, former Mayor G.T. Bynum, a Republican, transformed how the city used data to make decisions, and the approach was so effective that his Democratic successor, Mayor Monroe Nichols, has doubled down on Tulsa's citywide commitment to performance and accountability. In Denver, Mayor Johnston's focus on setting clear citywide goals and using data to track progress has helped the city break down departmental siloes and make meaningful progress on the city's toughest challenges.

Changing the "unwritten rules" of government—its practices, habits, and norms—to focus on what works is challenging, as Congressmen Greg Landsman and Rudy Yakym attest in their chapter. But it can be done, especially when leaders' first priority is orienting teams across government toward the results they need to achieve. Just look at San José, where Mayor Mahan is building a culture of innovation across city government, empowering thousands of employees to use AI to increase efficiency and improve residents' lives.

Perhaps the most important takeaway from this book is this: We know what it takes to do what works.

Through our fourteen years of leading Results for America, the field of government-improvement organizations has grown dramatically. Getting government to deliver is a complex challenge, and it requires strengthening government through better technology, better data, process improvements, and changes in civil service systems, like those being led by U.S. Digital Response, Code for America, Recoding America, the Data Quality Campaign, Partners for Public Good, the Partnership for Public Service, Work for America, and others. We have learned through our experience—and the chapters in this book demonstrate—that to fix government and deliver results for residents, it is essential to define the outcome and prioritize evidence and data, create incentives in public funding, and build a culture that supports all government decision-makers so they can focus on results, rather than inputs or government process.

The uncomfortable truth is that too many Americans are losing faith that their leaders will—or, indeed, *can*—get things done on their behalf. According to public polling from Pew Research Center, only 17 percent of Americans trust the federal government to do the right thing most of the time.[1] And 85 percent of Americans believe that elected officials simply do not care what people like them think.[2]

This decline in public trust undermines government's ability to rally support for the ambitious solutions needed to address our common challenges, most especially the decline in upward economic mobility and the fading American Dream. And when government is unable to address these kinds of big problems, it only reinforces people's sense that it is fundamentally not up to the job. It creates a vicious cycle.

This book proposes a solution to reverse that downward cycle. If government, everywhere, were to follow the examples of the leaders featured in these pages who are finding, funding, and doing what works, we firmly believe residents will begin to trust government again.

We recently partnered with Echelon Insights, led by pollster and *New York Times* contributor Kristen Soltis Anderson, to better understand Americans' views on evidence-based government, and whether it could help cross partisan divides to build trust in government. The results from the poll of a thousand likely voters were promising:

- Ninety-four percent of respondents said that evidence of what works should influence policymaking, with nearly identical support among Democrats and Republicans.
- Ninety-two percent of respondents agreed that using evidence would ensure that government makes progress instead of "doing the same things year after year."

- Eighty-five percent of respondents—clear majorities on both sides of the aisle—said they were more likely to vote for officials who supported policies that had been shown to work.[3]

Finally, and perhaps most promising, 89 percent said they believed that their trust in government could be rebuilt if leaders work to ensure programs are doing their intended jobs. In other words, if governments try to do what works.

We will leave you with a final "do what works" story that addresses a challenge facing many communities: rising eviction rates. In recent years, tenants across Los Angeles faced a surge in evictions driven by soaring rents, wages that have not kept pace, a shortage of affordable housing, and the lifting of Covid-era protections for tenants. Without help, tens of thousands of local residents and families each year were at risk of losing their homes.

Research from the Eviction Lab at Princeton University points to the serious economic and social consequences of eviction: Evicted families are often forced into worse housing and more disadvantaged neighborhoods; adults face job loss and financial instability; and children—who make up nearly 40 percent of those facing eviction—are more likely to change schools, miss classes, and be suspended. And even after the immediate crisis, an eviction record can follow tenants for years, damaging credit, limiting housing options, and driving up costs.[4]

Given the profound negative impacts of evictions on residents, city and county leaders in Los Angeles set a goal of strengthening housing stability for lower-income residents, and went searching for proven strategies to achieve it. They found inspiration in cities like New York and San Francisco, which had reduced evictions by adopting right-to-counsel ordinances guaranteeing legal representation to eligible tenants facing eviction. They began steering funding to what works by piloting increased access to counsel. In 2022, Los Angeles government leaders and their community partners joined other jurisdictions in a Results for America Solutions Sprint to help accelerate their implementation of a right to counsel for tenants. Within three years, both the city and county of Los Angeles passed ordinances and dedicated public funding to this solution.

Since 2021, more than thirty-three thousand Los Angeles residents have been helped, with eleven thousand receiving full legal representation. About half of all tenants receiving help were able to stay in their homes, while another 40 percent achieved "soft landings" that gave them additional time to move or avoid the long-term consequences of an eviction record. Previously, 99 percent of unrepresented tenants were disruptively displaced. In addition to helping people, this approach saves taxpayers money: For every dollar invested in this solution, the city and county save an estimated four dollars and fifty cents by avoiding more expensive costs, like providing emergency shelter to residents who experience homelessness.[5]

While the causes of rising evictions are often due to a complex mix of factors, Los Angeles government leaders and their partners in the community are steadily building a culture focused on preventing evictions and reducing harm to children and families today, opening opportunities for a longer-term solution.

Los Angeles is one example among hundreds where state and

local government leaders—like those in this book, from both political parties—are rejecting the status quo and finding, funding, and implementing effective, evidence-based solutions. They are innovating, adapting, and sharing what they learn with others. They are proving that progress is possible.

Beyond this book, it also is happening in Pennsylvania, where Democratic Governor Josh Shapiro and state leaders have invested in evidence-based workforce programs and secured universal free breakfast for 1.7 million students (increasing breakfast participation by 10 million meals in one year alone). "What people really want," he said, "is their elected leaders to be out there fixing something for them."

And it is happening in Utah, where Republican Governor Spencer Cox and his team worked hard to bring evidence-based budgeting to life. The Governor's Office of Planning and Budget issues budget request forms that require evidence of effectiveness for any desired funding, and agencies are required to set at least one performance metric for every approved budget request in excess of half a million dollars.

Governor Cox has also brought an evidence-driven approach to implementing the state's signature law tackling intergenerational poverty. He created an Office of Families, which has championed evidence-based investments like home visiting to improve health outcomes for moms and young children. The results are impressive: Child poverty has declined by 43 percent since 2012, and last year, Utah was ranked as the number-one state for social mobility, according to the Archbridge Institute.[6] As Governor Cox put it, "By keeping an open mind and letting the data guide us, I believe we've been able to make better decisions at every level of government."

And it is not just elected officials who demonstrate this kind of wisdom, commitment to results, and political courage on a daily basis.

It is public servants like Monica Dunleavy-Gerster in Chicago, whom you met in chapter 5, stepping up to the plate when a new process in her workflow required a steep learning curve but produced measurable results.

It is nonprofit leaders like Plinio Ayala, the CEO of Per Scholas, and Ruth Ann Moss, the executive director of Small Magic in Birmingham, who work collaboratively with local government leaders to fund and expand effective programs that are putting thousands of kids and adults on a path to success.

And it is private sector leaders like Dana Keller from the chamber of commerce, and her workforce specialist, Darlene Shopher, whose day-in, day-out efforts on behalf of workers in Audrain County, Missouri, are keeping more people employed.

There are people just like Monica, Plinio, Ruth Ann, Dana, and Darlene in every community in America—even those where there are not (yet) results-driven leaders in government. You probably know someone like them.

At a time when Washington is teetering between progress and retrenchment—the efforts of the bipartisan Congressional What Works Caucus notwithstanding—it is these state and local government leaders, as well as the nonprofit and private sector leaders who partner with them, who give us hope. Indeed, data- and evidence-driven government is coming from cities, counties, and states, from Democrats and Republicans and independents, from every level of government and every corner of the country.

We encourage you to join this movement. Share the stories in this book—and add your voice to the growing chorus of Americans who want results-driven government to be the rule, not the exception.

We know what it takes to do what works.

Let's now do it so that every person in our country has the opportunity to achieve their full potential.

ACKNOWLEDGMENTS

We are deeply indebted to all of the results-driven policymakers and nonprofit leaders (and their teams) featured in this book who shared stories of what is working in their communities. Serving at the highest levels of government is all-consuming, and yet each of these bipartisan leaders leaned into the opportunity to explain the urgent challenges their residents face and the solutions they are adopting. For their contributions—to this book and to the movement to build a government that works—we are immensely grateful.

We are also thankful to writer Andy Barr, whose gift for storytelling is reflected in every chapter. Our partners at Disruption Books, including Kris Pauls, Christina Pulles, and Janet Potter, have been instrumental at every step in bringing *Do What Works* from an idea to the book you hold in your hands. And our friend David Shipley offered thoughtful insights on the themes at the center of the book.

This book was inspired by the passion and optimism of Results for America's team. Many of the stories in the book come directly from our team's nonpartisan work with governors, mayors, county leaders, state legislators, and state school chiefs around the country. And our staff—including Zachary Coile, Ryan Galvin Wise, and others—collaborated closely with our government and nonprofit partners to bring each chapter to life.

Finally, we are thankful for you—our readers, partners, and supporters, both inside and outside of government, who share our belief in the power of evidence-based solutions to improve lives. You can find more examples like the ones highlighted in the book—and share some of your own—by visiting our Substack, *The Department of What Works.*

NOTES

Introduction

1. Marc J. Dunkelman, *Why Nothing Works: Who Killed Progress—and How to Bring It Back* (PublicAffairs, 2025).
2. Ezra Klein and Derek Thompson, *Abundance* (Simon & Schuster, 2025).
3. *Improving Elementary Literacy: The Power of Evidence-Based Investments by AmeriCorps* (Results for America, 2025), https://results4america.org/wp-content/uploads/2025/04/Reading-Corps-Case-Study-April-14-2025.pdf.
4. Center on Budget and Policy Priorities, "SNAP Helps Kids Over the Long Term, Too," Off the Charts (blog), Oct. 7, 2016, https://www.cbpp.org/blog/snap-helps-kids-over-the-long-term-too.
5. Dana Korsen, "Federal Tax Credits in 2021 Lifted More than 2 Million Children Out of Poverty, Says New Report," National Academies, Sept. 25, 2025, https://www.nationalacademies.org/news/federal-tax-credits-in-2021-lifted-more-than-2-million-children-out-of-poverty-says-new-report.
6. "The U.S. President's Emergency Plan for AIDS Relief (PEPFAR)," KFF, May 13, 2025, https://www.kff.org/global-health-policy/the-u-s-presidents-emergency-plan-for-aids-relief-pepfar/.

Chapter 2

1. Bishop Ken Untener, "The Romero Prayer," Nov. 1979, https://www.romerotrust.org.uk/romero-prayer/.
2. Stream and Wetlands Foundation, "H2Ohio Funding 2024 and 2025 State Fiscal Years," n.d., https://streamandwetlands.org/h2ohio/.
3. Ohio Department of Agriculture Staff, "Investing in Ohio's Water through H2Ohio," *Journal of Nutrient Management* (Nov. 2025): 22, https://jofnm.com/article-410-Investing-in-Ohio's-water-through-H2Ohio.html.
4. "Governor DeWine Announces H2Ohio Milestone: More than 200 Wetlands Complete or In-progress Statewide," Governor Mike DeWine (website), February 11, 2025, https://governor.ohio.gov/media/news-and-media/governor-dewine-announces-h2ohio-milestone-more-than-200-wetlands-complete-or-in-progress-statewide.
5. Ohio Department of Agriculture Staff, "Investing in Ohio's Water."

6. Ohio Department of Natural Resources, *Annual Report 2025*, https://dam.assets.ohio.gov/image/upload/odnr/department/2025_ODNR_Annual_Report.pdf.
7. Office of Governor Mike DeWine, "Governor DeWine Names Initial Communities Eligible for New Universal Nurse Home Visiting Program," news release, Apr. 12, 2024, https://governor.ohio.gov/media/news-and-media/governor-dewine-names-initial-communities-eligible-for-new-universal-nurse-home-visitng-program.
8. Ohio Governor's Office of Workforce Transformation, "Husted Announces Results for April Round of TechCred," news release, Jun. 4, 2021, https://workforce.ohio.gov/news/060321#:~:text=Lt%20Governor%20Jon%20Husted%20announced%20the%20results%20of%20the%20April%20TechCred%20application%20period%20today.
9. Ohio Department of Development, "Governor DeWine Announces Latest Awards From TechCred Program," news release, Nov. 25, 2025, https://development.ohio.gov/home/news-and-events/all-news/2025-1125-governor-dewine-announces-latest-awards-from-techcred-program.
10. Office of Governor Mike DeWine, "Governor DeWine Delivers 2025 State of the State Address," news release, Mar. 12, 2025, https://governor.ohio.gov/media/news-and-media/governor-dewine-delivers-2025-state-of-the-state-address.
11. Mike DeWine, "Ohio Gov. Mike DeWine offers State-of-the-State Address," *Richland Source*, Mar. 15, 2025, https://www.richlandsource.com/2025/03/15/ohio-gov-mike-dewine-offers-state-of-the-state-address/.
12. Mike DeWine, "Ohio Gov. Mike DeWine offers State-of-the State Address."
13. Mike DeWine, "Ohio Gov. Mike DeWine offers State-of-the State Address."
14. Scott Cohn, "America's Top States for Business: 2025: The full rankings," CNBC, July 10, 2025, https://www.cnbc.com/2025/07/10/top-states-for-business-americas-2025-the-full-rankings.html.

Chapter 3

1. Jennifer Ludden, "The Number of Homeless People in the U.S. Has Jumped to Another Record High," NPR, December 27, 2024, https://www.npr.org/2024/12/27/nx-s1-5240951/the-number-of-homeless-people-in-the-u-s-has-jumped-to-another-record-high.
2. U.S. Department of Veterans Affairs, "Veteran Homelessness Reaches Record Low, Decreasing by 7.5% Since 2023," VA News, November 12, 2024, https://news.va.gov/press-room/veterans-homelessness-reaches-record-low-decreasing-by-7-5-since-2023.
3. *Creating a Tipping Point for Solving Homelessness in the United States: 2024 Impact and Learning Report* (Community Solutions, 2024), https://community.solutions/download/impact-and-learning-2024/.
4. *Point in Time Report 2023: Denver County, Colorado* (Metro Denver Homeless Initiative, 2023), https://static1.squarespace.com/static/5fea50c73853910bc4679c13/t/64be8ba3c416ce515df1fdb3/1690209187980/Denver+County+PIT+Factsheet+2023.pdf.

5. Patrick Dawson, "Denver Crime Trends 2018–2022," Oct. 8, 2022, https://rpubs.com/pdawson12/956343; *Annual Report, 2022* (Office of the Medical Examiner, Denver Public Health & Environment, 2022), https://denvergov.org/files/assets/public/v/1/public-health-and-environment/documents/ome/2022annualreport.pdf.
6. Dana Ferrante et al., "Housing First Is Still the Best Approach to Ending Homelessness," Urban Institute's Housing Matters initiative, Feb. 14, 2024, https://housingmatters.urban.org/feature/housing-first-still-best-approach-ending-homelessness.

Chapter 4

1. Office of Governor Tate Reeves, "Governor Reeves Statement on Mississippi's Nation-leading NAEP Gains, Record Achievement," news release, Jan. 29, 2025, https://governorreeves.ms.gov/governor-reeves-statement-on-mississippis-nation-leading-naep-gains-record-achievement/.
2. Tate Reeves, "Governor Reeves Statement."
3. Horace Mann, "A Lecture on the Best Mode of Preparing and Using Spelling-Books," presented before the American Institute of Instruction, Aug. 1841, *Common School Journal* vol. 3–4 (1841): 9–16, 25–32.
4. National Institute of Child Health and Human Development, *Report of the National Reading Panel: Teaching Children to Read* (NIH Pub. No. 00-4769, April 2000), https://www.nichd.nih.gov/publications/pubs/nrp/smallbook.

Chapter 5

1. Rob Waters, "A Conversation With Tony D: How 'Becoming A Man' Got To The White House," *Forbes*, Mar. 9, 2016, https://www.forbes.com/sites/robwaters/2016/03/09/a-conversation-with-tony-d-how-becoming-a-man-got-to-the-white-house/.
2. J. J. Gallagher, "Aug. 2016: Chicago's Bloodiest Month in Two Decades," ABC News, Sept. 1, 2016, https://abcnews.com/US/aug-2016-chicagos-bloodiest-month-decades/story?id=41792681.
3. Sara B. Heller et al., "Thinking, Fast and Slow? Some Field Experiments to Reduce Crime and Dropout in Chicago," *Quarterly Journal of Economics* 132, no. 1 (Feb. 2017): 2, https://doi.org/10.1093/qje/qjw033.
4. Heller et al., "Thinking, Fast and Slow," 2.
5. Heller et al., "Thinking, Fast and Slow," 2.
6. "Innovator Interview: Lisa Morrison Butler, Chicago Department of Family and Support Services," Harvard Kennedy School Government Performance Lab, Mar. 17, 2021, https://govlab.hks.harvard.edu/insight/innovator-interview-lisa-morrison-butler-chicago-department-of-family-and-support-services/.
7. Scaling Promising Practices in Youth Mentoring (Results for America, 2023), https://results4america.org/wp-content/uploads/2023/10/RFA-Scaling-Promising-Practices-in-Youth-Mentoring-UPDATED-10-27.pdf.

8. *Enrollment Trends of the Mayor's Mentoring Initiative, September 2016–February 2018* (University of Chicago Urban Labs, 2018), https://educationlab.uchicago.edu/wp-content/uploads/sites/3/2023/07/2018-08-22_MMI-Report_vSENT_NoWatermark_V276.pdf.

Chapter 6

1. Philip Joens, "Effects of Factory Closure Still Linger," *Columbia Daily Tribune*, May 21, 2019, https://www.columbiatribune.com/story/news/local/2019/05/21/effects-factory-closures-still-linger/4893061007/.
2. Audrain County Missouri, "About Audrain County," n.d., https://www.audraincounty.org/about.
3. Ruby K. Payne, *A Framework for Understanding Poverty: A Cognitive Approach*, 6th ed. (aha! Process, 2019).
4. Ruby K. Payne, *Bridges Out of Poverty: Strategies for Professionals and Communities*, 5th ed. (aha! Process, 2021).
5. Jennifer Kuiper, "Chamber of Commerce Program Helps Keep Workers on the Job," National Association of Counties, Jan. 28, 2016, https://www.naco.org/news/chamber-commerce-program-helps-keep-workers-job-0.

Chapter 7

1. *The Science of Early Childhood Development* (Bipartisan Policy Center, n.d.), https://bipartisanpolicy.org/wp-content/uploads/2021/05/C.-1-The-Science-of-Early-Childhood.pdf.
2. Alaina Bookman, "Children Should Hear 21,000 Words a Day. A Birmingham Literacy Program Is Trying to Make that Happen," AL.com, Jul. 1, 2025, https://www.al.com/news/birmingham/2025/07/children-should-hear-21000-words-a-day-a-birmingham-literacy-program-is-trying-to-make-that-happen.html.
3. Laura J. Colker, "The Word Gap: The Early Years Make the Difference," *Teaching Young Children* 7, no. 3 (Feb./Mar. 2014), https://www.naeyc.org/resources/pubs/tyc/feb2014/the-word-gap.
4. James J. Heckman et al., "Lifecycle Benefit of an Influential Early Childhood Program (13% ROI)," The Heckman Equation, Dec. 19, 2016, https://heckmanequation.org/resource/13-roi-toolbox/.
5. City of Providence, Rhode Island, "Providence Talks Expands to Serve 750 Families Over the Next Year," news release, n.d., https://www.providenceri.gov/providence-talks-expands-serve-750-families-next-year/.
6. James Anderson, "What It Takes to Make City Solutions Go Viral," Bloomberg, Oct. 15, 2024, https://www.bloomberg.com/news/articles/2024-10-15/what-it-takes-to-make-city-solutions-go-viral.
7. Bookman, "Children Should Hear 21,000 Words a Day."

Chapter 8

1. John Kania and Mark Kramer, "Collective Impact," *Stanford Social Innovation Review* 9, no. 1: 36–41, https://doi.org/10.48558/5900-KN19.

2. "Cradle to Career," StriveTogether, n.d., https://www.strivetogether.org/what-we-do/cradle-to-career-outcomes/.

3. "Theory of Action Guiding Framework," StriveTogether, n.d., https://www.strivetogether.org/what-we-do/theory-of-action/.

4. Jennifer Blatz, "The Cradle to Career Network's Relentless Vision for 4 Million Futures," StriveTogether blog, Sept. 22, 2025, https://www.strivetogether.org/the-cradle-to-career-networks-relentless-vision-for-4-million-futures/.

5. Leah Binkovitz, "After 2011 Education Cuts, 'A Lost Half Decade'," Rice University Kinder Institute for Urban Research *Urban Edge* blog, Oct. 10, 2017, https://kinder.rice.edu/urbanedge/after-2011-education-cuts-lost-half-decade.

6. "An Urgent Call for Change in Texas Education," Commit Partnership, https://www.commitpartnership.org/about/history.

7. "Dallas County Sees Modest Increase in Young Adults Earning a Living Wage, But Gaps Persist," Commit Partnership blog, Mar. 11, 2026, https://www.commitpartnership.org/insights/latest-learnings/dallas-county-sees-modest-increase-in-young-adults-earning-a-living-wage-but-gaps-persist.

8. Yasser Kazzaz, "The Lens of Profound Knowledge," *Global Journal on Quality and Safety in Healthcare* 6, no. 3 (Aug. 24, 2023): 96–98, https://pmc.ncbi.nlm.nih.gov/articles/PMC10887482/#i2589-9449-6-3-96-b01.

9. Nicole Capó Martinez, "Using Data to Transform Futures in Dallas, Texas," StriveTogether blog, Dec. 14, 2023, https://www.strivetogether.org/using-data-to-transform-futures-in-dallas-texas/.

10. StriveTogether, "Delivering Equitable Education Finance Reform," 5.

11. StriveTogether, "Delivering Equitable Education Finance Reform," 4.

12. StriveTogether, "Delivering Equitable Education Finance Reform," 9.

13. "Dallas County Promise Celebrates Five-Year Anniversary, Plans to Expand to Support As Many As 28,000 Seniors Annually," Commit Partnership blog, Apr. 12, 2023, https://www.commitpartnership.org/insights/latest-learnings/dallas-county-promise-celebrates-five-year-anniversary-plans-to-expand-to-support-as-many-as-28-000-seniors-annually.

14. StriveTogether, "Delivering Equitable Education Finance Reform," 8.

15. Patrick Svitek, "Gov. Greg Abbott Signs $11.6 Billion School Finance Measure into Law," *Texas Tribune*, Jun. 11, 2019, https://www.texastribune.org/2019/06/11/texas-gov-greg-abbott-signs-116-billion-school-finance-measure-law/.

16. J. Jacob Kirksey et al., "From Incentive to Impact: The Texas Teacher Incentive Allotment's Path to Improved Retention and Achievement," Working Paper No. 02-001, Texas Tech University, Nov. 2024, https://ttu-ir.tdl.org/server/api/core/bitstreams/ff3bf151-b1e4-4872-9521-d7a3dc1b0e30/content.

17. *Students-First Policy Implementation in Texas: The 2024 Texas Impact Network Annual Report* (Impact Network, 2024), https://texasimpactnetwork.org/wp-content/uploads/2024/10/TIN-2024AnnualReport-20240924-V6-DIGITAL.pdf.

18. "Our History: An Urgent Call for Change in Texas Education," Commit Partnership, n.d., https://www.commitpartnership.org/about/history.

19. "Our Mission: Dallas County Has a Thriving Economy. But There's One Measure That Tells a Different Story," Commit Partnership, n.d., https://www.commitpartnership.org/impact/mission.

20. "Quotes Of The Day: India's Indira Gandhi On Beginning," *Investor's Business Daily*, Aug. 11, 2015, https://www.investors.com/news/management/wisdom-to-live-by/famous-quotes-by-jk-rowling-and-indira-gandhi/.

21. Matt Goodman, "How Big Data Turned an Empty South Dallas Lot Into a Vibrant Plaza," *D Magazine*, Jun. 8, 2022, https://www.dmagazine.com/frontburner/2022/06/how-big-data-turned-an-empty-south-dallas-lot-into-a-vibrant-plaza/.

22. Goodman, "How Big Data Turned an Empty South Dallas Lot."

23. Alan Cohen and Eric Johnson, "Violent Crime is Down in Dallas, and Here's Why," *Dallas Morning News*, Feb. 13, 2022, https://www.dallasnews.com/opinion/commentary/2022/02/13/violent-crime-is-down-in-dallas-and-heres-why/.

24. "CPAL Partner Spotlight: Dallas College," posted Jul. 31, 2025, by Child Poverty Action Lab, YouTube video, https://www.youtube.com/watch?v=Rog_kP0ZJIk.

25. "Eviction Statistics Dashboard," Dallas Eviction Advocacy Center, n.d., https://www.dallaseac.org/evictions-statistics-dashboard/#:~:text=Nearly%2040%2C000%20eviction%20cases%20are,in%20Dallas%20County%20each%20year.

26. "CPAL Partner Spotlight: Dallas Eviction Advocacy Center," posted Jul. 31, 2025, by Child Poverty Action Lab, YouTube video, https://www.youtube.com/watch?v=sPurSPMvBZ4.

Chapter 9

1. Monroe Nichols, "Mayor Nichols' Road to Repair," remarks given at Greenwood Cultural Center, Jun. 1, 2025, https://www.cityoftulsa.org/media/27976/mayor-nichols-road-to-repair.pdf.

2. Matt Trotter, "Study Finds Clear Reason for Disparities in Tulsa County Life Expectancies," Public Radio Tulsa, Sept. 3, 2015, https://www.publicradiotulsa.org/local-regional/2015-09-03/study-finds-clear-reason-for-disparities-in-tulsa-county-life-expectancies.

3. G.T. Bynum, "A Republican Mayor's Plan to Replace Partisanship with Policy," TED Talks, Feb. 2017, https://www.ted.com/talks/g_t_bynum_a_republican_mayor_s_plan_to_replace_partisanship_with_policy.

4. "Partisan Rhetoric Is for Losers | G.T. Bynum | TEDxPennsylvaniaAvenue," posted Mar. 1, 2017, by TEDx Talks, YouTube video, https://www.youtube.com/watch?v=GeD-gi0A7A8.

5. Sara Holder, "CityLab: The Data Brigade of Tulsa, Oklahoma," Results for America, Jul. 2, 2018, https://results4america.org/tools/citylab-data-brigade-tulsa-oklahoma/.

6. John Hope Franklin, "Rediscovering Black America: A Historical Roundup," *The New York Times*, Sept. 8, 1968, https://archive.nytimes.com/www.nytimes.com/books/99/08/15/specials/franklin-roundup.html.

7. Monroe Nichols, "2024 Inauguration Address" Dec. 2, 2024, https://www.cityoftulsa.org/media/26608/nichols-inaugural-address-pdf-12-2024.pdf.

Chapter 10

1. "About Per Scholas," Per Scholas, n.d., https://perscholas.org/about-per-scholas/.

2. "How AI is Redefining Entry-Level Tech Hiring," Per Scholas, February 17, 2026, https://enterprise.perscholas.org/how-ai-is-redefining-entry-level-tech-hiring/.

3. *Zero Percent Loan: Zero Interest, Zero Barriers—Transforming Workforce Access* (Per Scholas, n.d.), https://perscholas.org/wp-content/uploads/2024/12/Zero-Percent-Loan-Transforming-Workforce-Access.pdf.

4. *Unlocking Potential, Changing the Face of Tech: 2024 Annual Report* (Per Scholas, 2024), https://perscholas.org/2024-annual-report/.

5. "Joovay Arias," Per Scholas, n.d., https://perscholas.org/meet-our-graduates/story/joovay-arias/.

6. Dan Miner, "Why Per Scholas is Expanding in Buffalo," Series Buffalo, Feb. 16, 2026, https://www.seriesbuffalo.com/articles/why-per-scholas-is-expanding-in-buffalo.

7. "Lennon Williams," Per Scholas, n.d., https://perscholas.org/meet-our-graduates/story/lennon-williams/.

8. Carol Clymer et al., "Job Training That Works: Findings from the Sectoral Employment Impact Study," Public/Private Ventures, May 1, 2009, https://ppv.issuelab.org/resource/job-training-that-works-findings-from-the-sectoral-employment-impact-study.html.

9. *Tech Sector Career Training: Columbus, OH* (Results for America, Apr. 27, 2021), http://catalog.results4america.org/case-studies/job-training-columbus.

Chapter 11

1. *Workforce Pell: A New Opportunity for Tennesseans to Build Skills Through Short-Term Credentials* (TNScore.org, Jan. 2026), https://tnscore.org/assets/documents/Workforce-Pell-Memo-final.pdf.

2. Office of Governor Bill Lee, "Gov. Bill Lee Special Session Remarks as Prepared for Delivery," news release, Jan. 19, 2021, https://www.tn.gov/governor/news/2021/1/19/gov--bill-lee-remarks-as-prepared-for-delivery-on-special-session.html.

3. Laura Fay, "Student Survey: Despite High Numbers Saying Their Schools Were Assigning Work and They Were Completing it, Only Half Said They Were Really Learning During Pandemic," *The 74*, Jul. 22, 2020, https://www.the74million.org/article/student-survey-despite-high-numbers-saying-their-schools-were-assigning-work-and-they-were-completing-it-only-half-said-they-were-really-learning-during-pandemic/.
4. Tennessee Department of Education, "TDOE Releases 2022-23 State-Level TCAP Results," news release, Jun. 29, 2023, https://www.tn.gov/education/news/2023/6/29/tdoe-releases-2022-23-state-level-tcap-results-.html.
5. Karen Vaites, "The Southern Surge: Understanding the Bright Spots in the Literacy Landscape," *School Yourself*, Feb. 15, 2025, https://www.karenvaites.org/p/the-southern-surge-understanding.
6. Tennessee Department of Education, "Reading 360 Educator Training is Back, Bigger and Better for Summer 2022,"*Reading 360* Blog, May 24, 2022, https://www.tn.gov/education/reading-360/blog/2022/5/24/reading-360-educator-training-is-back-summer-2022.html.
7. Tennessee Department of Education, 2026.
8. Keenan Thomas, "Knox County Schools Improve in Grades from TN Education Department," *Knoxville News Sentinel*, Dec. 20, 2025, https://www.knoxnews.com/story/news/education/2025/12/20/knox-county-schools-improve-in-grades-from-tn-education-department/87824898007.
9. Tennessee Department of Education, "2025 TCAP District Results Dashboard," n.d., https://tdepublicschools.ondemand.sas.com/district/00440/assessment.
10. Jackson County School District, "Jackson County Schools was listed as 1 of the 10 school districts across the state of Tennessee for being an exemplary school district! Congratulations to the faculty and students for all their hard work and dedication!" news announcement, n.d., https://www.jacksoncoschools.com/apps/news/article/2037446?categoryId=13197.
11. Tennessee Department of Education, "National Assessment of Educational Progress (NAEP)," n.d., https://www.tn.gov/education/districts/lea-operations/assessment/naep.html.

Chapter 12

1. Matt Mahan, "Memorandum: March Budget Message for Fiscal Year 2023–2024," City of San José, Mar. 13, 2023, https://sanjose.legistar.com/View.ashx?M=F&ID=11736439&GUID=C8DF76A7-700D-49D0-8D26-2831051BA9F6.
2. Shawna Chen, "What SF Can Learn from San Jose's AI Deployment," *Axios San Francisco*, Sept. 30, 2025, https://www.axios.com/local/san-francisco/2025/09/30/san-jose-ai-permitting-potholes-sf-lessons.
3. Chen, "What SF Can Learn from San Jose's AI Deployment."

4. LYT, "Delivering Faster Bus Rides through Downtown San José," May 3, 2023, https://lyt.ai/customer-success-stories/delivering-faster-bus-rides-through-downtown-san-jose/; Diana Ionescu, "San José's Buses Run 20% Faster Thanks to AI," Planetizen, Feb. 9, 2026, https://www.planetizen.com/news/2026/02/136917-san-joses-buses-run-20-faster-thanks-ai.
5. "SJPD homicide unit has had 100% success rate for 3 years straight," posted May 19, 2025, by NBC Bay Area, YouTube video, https://www.youtube.com/watch?v=xOx5cPTPtlQ.
6. City of San José Office of the City Manager, "How the City is Increasing Community Safety," n.d., https://www.sanjoseca.gov/your-government/departments-offices/office-of-the-city-manager/city-council-focus-areas/increasing-community-safety.
7. City of San José, "San José AI Road Safety Pilot Data Shows 97% Accuracy," news release, Sept. 29, 2025, https://www.sanjoseca.gov/Home/Components/News/News/6926/4699.
8. City of San José, "San José City Clerk Launches Artificial Intelligence Initiative to Increase Language Access at City Council Meetings," news release, Apr. 29, 2024, https://www.sanjoseca.gov/Home/Components/News/News/5907/4699.
9. Jennifer Morrow, "Fact Brief: Does San Jose Have the Largest Vietnamese Population of Any City Outside of Vietnam?" *San José Spotlight*, Oct. 8, 2025, https://sanjosespotlight.com/fact-brief-does-san-jose-have-the-largest-vietnamese-population-of-any-city-in-the-world-outside-of-vietnam/.
10. City of San José Office of Economic Development and Cultural Affairs, "AI in San José: San José: Where Innovation Thrives and Leaders Converge," n.d., https://www.sjeconomy.com/how-we-help/programs-and-services/ai-start-up-incentive-program.
11. Kathleen Walch, "San José's Bold Plan To Lead The AI Revolution In City Government," *Forbes*, Sept. 20, 2025, https://www.forbes.com/sites/kathleenwalch/2025/09/20/san-joss-bold-plan-to-lead-the-ai-revolution-in-city-government/.
12. Matt O'Brien, "San Jose Mayor Uses AI for Work," Associated Press, Jul. 17, 2025, https://sanjosespotlight.com/san-jose-mayor-uses-ai-artificial-intelligence-chat-gpt-for-work/.
13. Metropolitan Transportation Commission Programming and Allocations Committee, "MTC Resolution Nos. 3989, Revised; 4202, Revised; 4505, Revised; and 4540, Revised," Mar. 12, 2025, https://mtc.ca.gov/sites/default/files/meetings/attachments/6248/2c_25_0257_1_Summary_Sheet_OBAG_2_3_CRP_MTC_Resolution_No_4505_Revised.pdf.
14. City of San José Department of Energy, "Mobility: Electric Vehicles," updated July 2025, https://www.sanjoseca.gov/your-government/departments-offices/energy/climate-smart-san-jose/climate-smart-data-dashboard/mobility-electric-vehicles.
15. Sophia Fox-Sowell, "AI Now Powers Street Hazard Detection in San Jose, Calif.," *Statescoop*, Sept. 29, 2025, https://statescoop.com/san-jose-ai-street-hazard-detection/.
16. Jule Pattison-Gordon, "San Jose Wants Its Workforce to Make Their Own AI Assistants," *Governing*, Jul. 21, 2025, https://www.governing.com/management-and-administration/san-jose-wants-its-workforce-to-make-their-own-ai-assistants.
17. City of San José, "Generative AI Guidelines," last updated Apr. 24, 2025, https://www.sanjoseca.gov/home/showpublisheddocument/100095/638811146637000000.

18. Walch, "San José's Bold Plan."

Chapter 13

1. Evidence-Based Grantmaking Act, H.R. 7025, 119th Cong. (2025).
2. *The Promise of Evidence-Based Policymaking: Report of the Commission on Evidence-Based Policymaking* (Commission on Evidence-Based Policymaking, Sept. 2017), https://www2.census.gov/adrm/fesac/2017-12-15/Abraham-CEP-final-report.pdf.
3. Evidence-Based Grantmaking Act, H.R. 7025, 119th Cong. (2025).
4. Office of Congressman Rudy Yakym, "Taxpayer Dollars Should Go to What Works, Not What Wastes," news release, Jan. 15, 2026, https://yakym.house.gov/posts/rep-yakym-taxpayer-dollars-should-go-to-what-works-not-what-wastes.
5. *Loper Bright Enterprises et al. v. Raimondo, Secretary of Commerce, et al.*, Volume 603 U.S. Part 1, https://www.supremecourt.gov/opinions/23pdf/22-451_7m58.pdf.

Conclusion

1. "Public Trust in Government: 1958–2025," Pew Research Center, December 4, 2025, https://www.pewresearch.org/politics/2025/12/04/public-trust-in-government-1958-2025/.
2. "More than 80% of Americans believe elected officials don't care what people like them think," Pew Research Center, April 30, 2024, https://www.pewresearch.org/short-reads/2024/04/30/more-than-80-of-americans-believe-elected-officials-dont-care-what-people-like-them-think/.
3. "Poll: American Attitudes Toward Evidence-Based Policymaking," Results for America, February 2026, https://results4america.org/evidence-based-policymaking-poll/.
4. "Eviction Lab Research," Eviction Lab, June 4, 2025, https://evictionlab.org/research/.
5. Jadeen Samuels, "Tenants Have Long Been at a Disadvantage in Eviction Court. Los Angeles is Changing That," *The Department of What Works*, April 28, 2026, https://thedepartmentofwhatworks.substack.com/p/tenants-have-long-been-at-a-disadvantage.
6. Justin T. Callais, Vincent Geloso, and Gonzalo Schwarz, "Social Mobility in the 50 States: 2025 Edition," Archbridge Institute, November 13, 2025, https://www.archbridgeinstitute.org/social-mobility-in-the-50-states/.

ABOUT THE AUTHORS

Editors Michele Jolin and David Medina are the Co-Founders of Results for America, a national nonprofit that helps government leaders find, fund, and implement solutions that work to accelerate upward economic mobility and improve lives.